Philosophy in Science Library

Editors: M. Heller and J. Zycinski

Volume 1
The World and the Word:
Between Science and Religion
by Michael Heller

Philosophy in Science Library

General Editors: M. Heller and J. Zycinski

THE WORLD AND THE WORD:
Between Science and Religion
Michael Heller. Translated by A. Chester Kisiel.
For those who have grown up in the positivistic tradition religious faith is impossible not so much as contrary to particular conclusions of science, but rather as having been eliminated by the expansion of scientific methods to all areas of human activity. The author demonstrates that such a position is itself based on an act of irrational faith. He lucidly examines the possibility of faith in the modern world dominated by methods and attainments of sciences.
(Philosophy in Science Library, Volume 1)
ISBN 0-88126-724-4 $ 14.95

THE CATASTROPHIC UNIVERSE:
An Essay in the Philosophy of Cosmology
A. G. Pacholczyk
Professor Pacholczyk presents the historical development of cosmology through a series of catastrophes, with new cosmological outlooks invalidating and replacing earlier ones, rather than through correspondent generalizations, and critically examines recent observations that imply potential new catastropheic changes at the cosmological level in the future. A philosophy of cosmology is considered in the final chapter, emphasizing the limitations inherent in cosmology as a discipline.
(Philosophy in Science Library, Volume 2)
ISBN 0-88126-702-3 $ 9.95

THE STRUCTURE OF THE META-SCIENTIFIC REVOLUTION
An Essay on the Growth of Modern Science
Joseph M. Zycinski
Revolutions occur not only on the level of scientific investigations but also on the level of epistemological and methodological reflection. Analyzing transformations in the paradigm of contemporary physics and mathematics the author points out falsification of some methodological doctrines. The new meta-scientific solutions must not be treated as a proclamation of an "absolute relativism" but rather as a new scientific paradigm free of uncritical dreams of the past.
(Philosophy in Science Library, Volume 3)
ISBN 0-88126-703-1 $ 48.00

THE WORLD AND THE WORD

Between Science and Religion

Michael Heller

Translated by Adam Chester Kisiel

Pachart Publishing House
Tucson

Michael Heller (1936-   )
The World and the Word:
Between Science and Religion

Library of Congress Catalog Card Number: 86-061668
International Standard Book Number: 0-88126-724-4

Philosophy in Science Library Volume 1

Pachart Publishing House
A Division of Pachart Foundation
A Nonprofit Association
1130 San Lucas Circle
P. O. Box 35549
Tucson, Arizona 85704

Contents

Introduction:

The World and the Word

In the first cell which inaptly began to pulsate with life the future expansion of living organisms was already coded. Very quickly the entire planet was enveloped by the biosphere as by an overcoat.

History repeated itself once again when the spark of preconsciousness flashed in the mind of primaeval man. The prospects of conquest were even more stunning: the field of human thought - the logosphere -now reaches beyond the solar system to the stars and galaxies. Man created the sciences in order to understand the Universe which surrounds him and of which he is a part. The sciences are an undertaking which man has taken up in answer to the challenge of the Universe.

The logosphere permeates the Universe. But the logosphere has a more complicated structure than the Universe. The logosphere includes not only the region controlled by the sciences, but also everything that can be termed the spiritual culture of man.

The word "Logos" seems particularly apt here, replete as it is with the import of history:

Logos - the word which expresses thought.

Logos - the thought which can be expressed in a word.

Logos - logically organized cognition (logic, cosmology, psychology, etc.).

Logos - the Word which was at the beginning and which became flesh (from the prologue to St. John),

and many other shades of meaning.

The question often referred to by the provocative slogan of "science and faith" belongs to the internal problems of the structure of the logosphere. Whitehead did not hesitate to write: "When we consider what religion is for mankind, and what science is, it is no exaggeration to say that the future course of history depends upon the decision of this generation as to the relations between them" (Science and the Modern World).

The considerations in this book grew out of personal experience. The areas of my personal activity are closely connected with both religion and science. I became a priest because I wanted to give people what is most important for them; I began to cultivate science in order... to know. But I do not treat science as a sideline. This cannot succeed. Science is such that either one devotes oneself completely to it or one achieves nothing in it. And so in this way somewhere within me there took place the clash of two fields that require complete committal. This is precisely my experience.

Part of this experience undoubtedly consists in conversations. Conversations with my colleagues, priests and scientists. The former I often provoked into replying, the latter, it seems, were sufficiently provoked by the fact that I found myself in their midst. My considerations are devoted to both of them. I devote them to priests, for they generally much too facilely discourse on the problems of science and faith; I devote them to scientists, for very often they are unable to solve these problems. Perhaps these considerations will be an extension of our never-finished conversations.

The reading of books and articles are also conversations. Very valuable ones. I owe much to them. All the more so in that sometimes it is not enough to exchange ideas; one simply has to learn many things. For this reason also, many chapters of this book are relations "second hand", reports from readings, but reports within the broad context of my own thoughts.

The case with readings is like that with acquaintances among people. On the whole, one does not choose one's acquaintances but meets them, and then only from among those whom one has met does one choose those with whom one wishes to maintain social contacts. I did not have a plan of readings laid out in advance but rather carefully searched among books for those which could help me in my considerations; among those which I read I selected only those which essentially enriched my chain of argumentation.

I am aware that this will not be easy reading matter. Philosophers and theologians will find in it a thread closer

10

to the style (as concerns both form and content) of the empirical sciences; readers with training in the empirical sciences will encounter a chain of argumentation expressed, perhaps, in a philosophical language alien to them. I did not intend to write a popular book. I encountered a difficult set of problems of great importance. It seems to me that I could have said something new or at least in a still unexploited way. Perhaps the time for popularization will come later.

But I do not wish to discourage the Reader at the very outset. Despite everything, I did not write for those who with the same routine can read St. Thomas Aquinas, Kant, and Einstein (if such exist at all, then the reading of my book would most probably be superfluous for them). I only ask the Reader not to put the book aside too readily should he be discouraged by encountering several unfamiliar terms. I believe that the general line of reasoning can be understood even without grasping several less important details.

In the Introduction I still owe the Reader several explanations of a more "technical" nature. First, the element of the relation "science-religion" can be religion in general or each religion separately. In the book, even if I speak of religion in general, I have in mind as an example or as a special case the Christian religion. This has its justification both for obvious personal reasons as well as for more general reasons: science came into being within the circle of culture shaped and permeated by Christianity. Historically speaking, Christian thought was the "antecedent" of science.

Second, strictly speaking, the relation "science-religion" is a cryptonym designating the whole network of relations between the following elements: knowledge, reason, science, the philosophy of science, and so on, on the one hand, and belief, religion, theology, meta-theology, etc., on the other hand. Here one should remember that each of these elements has many different meanings. Nowhere in the book have these meanings been systematically defined. I did not want to transform the book into a sterile study of meanings and classification of terms. I believe that the context and the supplying of sufficient explanations where necessary protects the line of argument from ambiguity.

And finally, third, the book does not aim at proving the truthfulness or supernaturality of the Christian religion. For that reason, when in the fourteenth chapter the question arises on the truthfulness of faith (its rational justification), the answer is postponed for another occasion. On the other hand, the aim of the book is to consider the

11

possibility of faith in the world of modern culture dominated by the methods and attainments of the sciences. For many people living in this world, and having consciously or unconsciously grown up in the positivistic tradition, religious faith is simply impossible not so much as contrary to some conclusions of science, but rather as eliminated by the expansion of scientific methods to all areas of human activity. The book shows that such a position is based on an act of irrational faith.

Of course, I do not believe that my considerations close the problem. Today more than ever before one should be aware that our epoch is the only link which has its raison d'etre solely in the fact that it is stretched between the past and that which is to come.

1

ANTINOMIES

First one must understand the roots of the problem. One cannot yield to the temptation of skimming the surface. It is generally regarded that the problem of science and faith only appeared in modern times. Why, earlier there were no science? True, but the modern sciences did not grow out of nothing; they have their roots in the most ancient strata of human thought. And if one is to understand the conflict of science and faith more broadly, as the encounter of human thought with Revelation, then this conflict is as old as religion.

The first chapter presents the history (and prehistory, that is, the period before the appearance of the sciences) of the problem of science and faith.

But one cannot stop with history. In popular versions of the conflict writers most often leave off at the stage of nineteenth century debates and polemics, when this clash took place between the accelerating, but still mechanistic sciences, and theology, which was then notoriously lagging behind contemporary problems. In the interim, far reaching changes have taken place: on the one hand, science has irrevocably moved away from mechanism and created reflections on itself, or the philosophy of science; on the other hand, theology has clearly greatly quickened its pace. The relations between science and theology have entered a qualitatively new phase.

The second chapter discusses the contemporary state of the problem.

Both in history as well as in analysis of the contemporary state of the problem, science, usually more or less theoretically conceived, is regarded as an opponent of religion (or theology). Tensions are noted between some features of religion and the scientific picture of the world. Meanwhile, science today, more than ever before, has practical meaning. Thanks to its offshoot - technology, it not only studies the world but also transforms it. The technological consequences of science made a much stronger impression on the mentality of the vast majority of people than its purely theoretical achievements.

The third chapter discusses the tension of science and faith in the climate of the rapid advances of modern technology.

All three chapters of the first part aim at a proper understanding of the problem provocatively termed "science and faith". The proper formulation of a problem is very often its partial solution. For that reason, the reading of the first part may already stimulate thoughts, leading, perhaps, in the right direction.

One:

Antinomies of Development

1. Instead of an Introduction, a Confusion of Tongues.

This chapter touched off a heated debate before it was written. I gave the rough draft to many people to read. The disputants divided themselves into two classes: "theologians" and "scientists". It turned out that the common part of these classes was an empty class. The significance of this fact I leave without comment.

In the rough draft I wrote: "I pose the thesis that the central problem of Christian theology is the problem of science and faith. If one treats this problem most broadly, as the confrontation of human thought with something that asserts that it is revealed truth, then every theology is derived therefrom." "Theologians" (people who in one way or another have been in closer contact with the study of theology) immediately came out with a whole series of objections.

"I do not know whether the first of those statements is correct, but one certainly should not identify human thought with science, as the second statement asserts. For me science is not even the most important element of human thought."

"I question this thesis - it is only one of the forms of the problem."

"This thesis is positively incorrect. In the act of faith man does not stand before God equipped with his entire scientific apparatus. Faith is an existential answer, complete engagement, and not a discursively drawn conclusion."

"It is not science that is the main problem for faith. In the majority of cases the basic motive for the lack of faith in God is not the fact that faith in Him would be contradictory with some accepted scientific statement. This can always be reconciled in one way or another. The basic problem is the existence of evil. The difficulty is not faith in God, but faith in a good God. Thus not the problem of science, but the problem of history intertwined with evil... " Etc., etc.

On the other hand, "scientists" (people in one way or another connected with cultivation of the exact sciences) did not have any essential objections to the content of the thesis posed by me. Some of them would have preferred a different formulation, but they agreed that in the acceptance or rejection of religious faith the element of confrontation of "scientific knowledge" with religious faith plays an essential role with them.

The problem of science and faith has as many shades of meaning and as many contexts as there were, are, and will be people experiencing this problem. "Professional deformation" must occur, but mutual accusations of ignorance solve nothing (that scientists have not the faintest idea of theology; that theologians enter the discussion without even knowing what Newton's second principle is). What I shall here set forth will certainly be in my "shade" and from the position of "my context". It cannot be otherwise, and, after all, under any other assumptions my understanding would be lacking in any value whatsoever from the very outset.

2. Collision.

I shall not argue whether the problem of science and faith is the central, one of the central, or only a very important problem of theology. Nonetheless, I support the assertion that each theology derives from the encounter of human thought with something that concerning itself asserts that it is revealed truth. This formulation requires, as the discussion showed, commentary. In order to resolve the first misunderstanding: it is not religion that derives from the encounter of human thought with revelation, but theology. And again, I do not intend to enter into the debates and discussions on the subject of the definition and methodological status of theology, but whatever definition of theology we might accept, we always assume that it is an attempt at reflection, some sort of attitude, an effort to define one's own relation to, in a word, the encounter of human thought with, revelation. This can be an encounter "under various aspects": axiological, anthropological, ethical, or other which already depends on the theology in question and on the position which it takes, but one way or another there are two sides: human thought and that SOMETHING which it encounters.

Thought penetrates all areas of human activity, but certainly science, in contemporary understanding of the term, is one of the most beautiful efflorescences of the thought of man. (I would write the most beautiful, but then what would e.g. poets, writers, artists say?) "Human thought" today is more than ever before shaped by the language, and even by the specific achievements, of various sciences. And for this reason an important, and perhaps continually growing, role in the theological problems of modern man is played by the scientific component of human thought.

One of my discussants asserted that the "central" problem of theology is not the conflict with human thought, but the problem of evil. Precisely! When I say: "The existence of evil contradicts the existence of God", this enters into conflict with my, still perhaps only potential, faith and my knowledge resulting from the experience of evil. When a father looks at the undeserved sufferings of his child, his heart rebels in him. Rebellion of the heart is not simultaneously a rebellion of thought for only those people among whom the heart has completely taken over the functions of the mind.

What is more, even such elementary experiences of man as the experience of evil are more and more often expressed in language borrowed from science. This same discussant of mine said: "The fact of evolution always filled me with outright freaks with two backbones and undeveloped brains, children dying as a result of a deficient arrangement of genes, the price which one has to pay for evolution to go forward, all of this blocks the way to faith in a good God. And a not-good-God is not a God at all." A typical situation: faith in God is confronted with a certain scientific theory extrapolated far beyond the area of its proper application; in this case the theory of evolution extended from the biological sciences up to the regions of the meaning of life and attempting to "explain" the existence of evil as a price for evolutionary benefits. This is an example of the conflict between human thought and the problem which eludes it.

3. Content and Form of Expression.

The conflict of science and faith is not unique to modern times. It appeared much earlier in various forms. Before the true sciences appeared (and then also parallel to sciences), human thought in this conflict was represented by various presciences (or near sciences), i.e. philosophy, common sense, etc. As we have seen the seeds of the conflict inhere in the very essence of theology.

Let us go back to the beginning. Christianity appeared in an epoch and in a region dominated by Graeco-Roman culture. To be sure, it had at its disposal the entire Old Testament and Judaic tradition from which it emerged and in which it was rooted, but - firstly - strictly speaking this tradition was never a product completely isolated from what was happening around it, and - secondly - in the times when Christianity appeared one absolutely can no longer speak of Judaic culture without considering Graeco-Roman influences.

A conflict occured. On the one hand, Christianity had to express itself through the language of the Judeo-Graeco-Roman culture which it found, and, on the other hand, Judeo-Graeco-Roman culture could not remain indifferent to new, Christian contents. Today, after the unquestionable achievements of analytical and hermeneutic philosophy, we understand better than ever before how much the content depends on the language through which it is expressed. The essence of the conflict, as I believe, consisted in a certain tension between the deepest content of the Christian doctrine and the conceptual and linguistic apparatus through which this doctrine had to express itself.

The flagrant polemics which took place between the representatives of pagan philosophy and the apologists of the young Christianity, or the debates among Church writers themselves on the subject of the proper attitude toward "Greek wisdom" were merely a consequence and an outward sign of that basic conflict: between the transcendental content and the means of expression at its disposal.

Toward the end of antiquity Greek wisdom gave up its place in the historical arena to Christian wisdom, but it passed on to Christianity its conceptual framework, or in any case the philosophical substance from which such a framework could further be developed. Human thought pitted itself against Revelation and entered into its very conceptual formulation. And that is how it remained. This form of conflict cannot be avoided. In whatever language, through whatever conceptual arrangements we might wish to apprehend Revelation there will always be an abysmal lack of proportion between the content and the means of expression at our disposal. The conflict did not end in 313 with the Edict of Milan.

4. The Limits of Reason and the Limits of Faith.

From the moment when Revelation already became dressed in an ever more complicated system of concepts, sooner or later the question on the limits of competence had to arise: How far do the limits of independent philosophical thought extend? Where does "reflection in the light of Revelation" or theology, supervised by the Church authority begin? Besides, the very distinction between philosophy and theology emerged only gradually in the painful polemics and disputes of the early Middle Ages. Clear boundaries were not drawn before St. Albert the Great (1193 - 1280) and St. Thomas Aquinas (1225 or 1227 - 1274). The field of unfettered reasoning is called philosophy; where reason can only begin to operate when it is supported by the "light of Revelation" is the starting point of theology. Philosophy is to be the "handmaid of theology", but it has already been detached from it as an independent discipline.

As we know, boundaries are often the object of disputes, especially if they pass between countries which have just gained autonomy. When it came to concrete determinations as to which truths belonged to philosophy and which to theology, views were divided and in a state of constant evolution. St. Thomas himself stipulated, in a cerain sense, a balance of forces between philosophy and theology: there exists a whole series of non-revealed truths which we discover through reason (so-called secular sciences); there exist revealed truths which reason can never discover (mysteries of faith) and revealed truths which we can also discover through philosophical reasoning, for example: the existence of God, His attributes (omnipotence, absoluteness,...), the immortality of soul, free will, and others. But already Duns Scotus (1270 - 1308) narrowed the field accessible to reason. In his opinion through pure reason we can demonstrate that God exists and that He created the world, but we can only believe in the attributes of God and the immortality of soul. William

Ockham (1300 - 1350) went even further. In doubting the principle of causality, he had to reject the evidential validity of all existing arguments for the existence of God, and hence move even this truth to the area of faith. Since in the area of faith reason is completely powerless, for Ockham theology completely ceased to be a science.

Neither Duns Scotus, nor William Ockham, nor - in general - any of their contemporaries believed that the assertions of faith were false; on the contrary, they remained true believers and only thought that these assertions could not be demonstrated through reason. It would seem that the process of limiting the competency of reason in the area of faith was a systematic phenomenon throughout the whole Middle Ages. Thomas, Duns Scotus, Ockham are only its milestones. Long before the natural sciences appeared, theological scepticism, practically speaking, had led to complete separation between science and faith.

5. Scientific and Ideological Revolutions.

Modern times. The empirical sciences enter the scene. Never before had human thought achieved such astounding successes. The historical law of the struggle of the old with the new somehow automatically set philosophy and theology against the young sciences. We usually have this stage in mind when we speak of the dispute between "science and faith". The "issue of Copernicus" and the "issue of Darwin" were highpoints of the conflict and became, as it were, symbols of the problem.

I like Karl Popper's distinction between scientific and ideological revolutions. "Ideology" in this context means "any non-scientific theory or creed or view of the world which proves attractive, and which interests people including scientists". Scientific revolutions consist in replacing some existing scientific theory with a new, more general theory which is in accord with the old empirical facts (explained by the old theory) and with the new ones (not fitting into the framework of the old theory). An ideological revolution is a turn in some generally accepted non-scientific views. A scientific revolution is always "rational" in character; there are logical criteria of progress in science. Ideological revolutions can also sometimes be "rational", but "we do not seem to have anything like general criteria of progress or of rationality outside science" (1).

Sometimes there are mutual influences between scientific and ideological revolutions. In the Copernican and Darwinian cases the scientific revolution initiated an ideological revolution. The revolutions of Copernicus and Darwin are ideological revolutions, since both of them changed the view of people on their place in the Universe; they are also scientific revolutions, since both one and the other replaced generally accepted existing theories in astronomy and biology, respectively.

In antiquity, Christianity was "something new"; in the Middle Ages the dispute took place inside the Church; in modern times Church doctrine stood in opposition to "something new", which emerged in an area independent of it. Antiquity gave birth to theology, the Middle Ages turned it into a total system; modern times questioned the reason for its existence.

I believe that what happened in the sixteenth and seventeenth centuries has irreversible consequences to this day. In previous centuries the Church performed the role of an International, or, rather, a Supranational Academy of Sciences. Because of this the scientific authority - if one can so express oneself - of the Church (along with the clergy) was enormous. At the beginning of modern times the Church lost this trump card completely. From then on there existed parallel secular and Church educational systems; many of the most outstanding scientists openly professed their affiliation to the Church, but it is an undisputed fact that scientific progress occured independently of the Church, outside the area of its direct influences. The division between the "world of the Church" and the "world of science" became ever greater, and more and more changed into total separation. If some fleeting contacts took place, they most often had the character of brief conflicts.

The Middle Ages introduced the distinction between philosophy and theology, but despite everything philosophy was understood mainly as an instrument for deepening theological investigations. The imposing theological edifice of the Middle Ages led to the obliteration of transitorial stages between Revelation itself and its theological formulation and between theology and philosophy in the intellectual life of the Church (in theory highly sensitive to these distinctions!). Traditional philosophy was too far advanced in its scholastic evolution in order to adapt to the changed natural environment which the scientific climate of Europe at that time became for it. The instinct of self-preservation set the mechanism of isolation into motion.

21

In theology and "Church philosophy" progress continued; but this was a progress without visible influences on the shape of cultural environment.

In the nineteenth century the Church lost the working class; the loss of the scientific intelligentsia was already a foregone conclusion at the turn of the sixteenth and seventeenth centuries. It is possible that the second loss (the working class) was a consequence of the first (loss of the scientific-technical intelligentsia) (2).

Meanwhile, science more and more became a supranational institution, while its authority - all the greater in that it was not encased in clear external forms - to a certain extent replaced the former authority of the Church. The picture of the world suggested by the empirical sciences is today nearly as obligatory for an educated person as religious dogmas for a believer.

To be sure, there were attempts to build bridges or to create a dialogue between "Church thought" and "scientific thought". An example of such an attempt is neo-Thomism at the end of the nineteenth and beginning of the twentieth centuries. An instructive example: the attempt to catch up to modernity became a succesive stage of the development taking place in tight isolation from the "rest of the world".

The second Vatican Council, and still more the theologians of the post-council period called attention to this isolation. Many attempts, some of them quite radical, were undertaken to translate theology into modern language. In their effort to cross the isolating barrier "Church philosophers" and theologians borrowed from non-Catholic theologians and "secular philosophers". And so Thomism gave way to Christianized versions of existentialism, phenomenology, structuralism, etc.; all of this seasoned with historicism and sociologism. The neglect of several centuries cannot be made up in the life of one generation. But something is happening. And this fills us with optimism. Limited optimism, however... To greatly simplify the matter (the whole time I am only sketching the broad outlines) one can agree with the assertion that the humanistic sciences are gradually beginning to carry weight in "Church thought". And as far as the exact empirical sciences are concerned... Some theologians believe that the interest in Teilhardism is the result of a longing for the "synthesis of the natural sciences", but Teilhardism is a vision of the world which really has little in common with the empirical sciences.

In the past some scientific theory could threaten some dogma of faith. Today science as a whole seems to threaten the existence of religion itself. Not by denying it or by combatting it; simply by not leaving it a place in the picture of the world which it draws. In any case, such is the psychological effect in the minds of many people cultivating science and in the minds of the broad circles of the technical intelligentsia.

I wish to end this part of my reflection with two reservations. Firstly, I have drawn above a very simplified sketch of the development of the relations beteen science and religion; my intention was not to write a historical study, but to grasp several regularities which would form the base for further considerations. Secondly, in essence this sketch concerned the relations between science as an institution and religion as an institution. Dependencies which reach deeper, under the layer of institutionalization, reveal the positive role of the Christian religion in the process of the development of science. More recent historical studies stress that it was precisely thought based on Christian Revelation which created a climate in which a scientific revolution could be set in motion at the beginning of modern times, while medieval philosophy was a necessary forerunner of revolutionary changes. Since I intend to return to this problem, in the meantime I refer the Reader to a reference in which he will find introductory bibliographical guides (3).

6. Pseudo-Dogmas and Scientific Progress.

It is indisputable fact that in the history of our culture the process of the maturation and emancipation of science was accompanied by the process of the laicization of intellectual life. Is this a chance convergence caused by "initial conditions" of the history of culture, or is it also an essential convergence, a connection resulting from the nature of things? It is difficult to answer this question unequivocally. We only have one example of the formation and development of empirical sciences (other human cultures did not create sciences so highly advanced), and making statistics on one example makes no sense. The example of our culture demonstrates only a certain kind of difference between the empirical sciences and religious cognition. The separation of the "community of scientists" from the "community of priests" is the manifestation of a more basic difference of methods and the nature of empirical and religious cognition.

Recognition of the difference between the two areas of cognition is not a priori equivalent with denying one of them

23

the right to exist. Totalistic tendencies of one side or the other lead to the danger of a narrowing of intellectual horizons and in extreme cases to scientific or fideistic obscurantism. Furthermore, this kind of fatalism proves unsuccessful. The history of our culture and civilization demonstrates this.

And still one lesson from this history. Science has autonomy in relation to religion. Whatever kind of interference of religious authorities (dogmas or hierarchy) in intrascientific assertions always proved fatal for those authorities and in the long run never had any real influence on the development of science. On the other hand, theology (or, more generally speaking, reasoned reflection on the content of religious faith) is not independent from the development of science. The interpretation of the content of religious faith is so deeply rooted in the picture of the world conventional in a given epoch that not infrequently it takes elements of this picture for revealed truth (e.g. the immovability of the Earth in the pre-Copernican picture of the world). The development of science, which introduces revolutionary changes or corrections in the conventional picture of the world, permits us to eliminate these kinds of pseudo-dogmas from the set of religious assertions. This is the important purifying role of science in relation to theology. In this connection one sometimes speak of the demythologization of theology by the positive sciences. Such intervention may be accompanied by painful blows to theologians, but - firstly - the matter concerns the honesty of theology itself, and - secondly - only then will theology have a chance to speak to the man of the future.

7. Theology and Invariants.

Two dangers are connected with the program of purification or demythologization of theology: (1) a priori suspecting that the process of purification is a latent departure from faith, and (2) regarding everything in theology as myth-legends. The first danger results from profound misunderstanding of the necessity for a well conceived purification of theology; the second is a groundless extremity. Here I should like to employ a comparison from geometry. A geometrical object (e.g. vector) is an entity independent from the selection of the system of coordinates, but if we wish to perform "operations" with it (make calculations), we must use coordinates which - as their name suggests are essentially dependent on the system of coordinates. The same geometrical object has various coordinates in various systems of coordinates (in various systems of reference when we speak of physical applications); one can even define it as something which does not change when its coordinates change with the passage to a new system of coordinates. We say that a geometrical object is an invariant of this or another transformation of coordinates. In geometrical physical theories (e.g. in the general theory of relativity) as a rule we encounter situations in which we can only measure coordinates, while we construct invariants through calculation (we can find an invariant only if we know its coordinates in at least two different frames of reference). I believe that in theology we have a similar situation. Here there exist certain Invariants, only we never have direct access to them (Mysteries of Faith), but only through the mediation of a certain "language of coordinates", which is strictly dependent of the "system of reference" with which the theologian is connected, i.e. with the past and the cultural, philosophical context, scientific picture of the world, language, conception of theology, etc. All attempts at demythologizing are only a passage from one "language of coordinates" to another "language of coordinates", from one "frame of reference" to another "frame of reference". The theologian never has access to the Invariants themselves, but such a passage to new "system of reference" is a necessary operation in order to glimpse the existence of Invariants at all.

During the last centuries up to the age of Pius XII theologians worked almost exclusively in one "system of reference" (Thomistic theology) and for that reason were inclined to absolutize it; everything which appeared in this "system of reference" seemed to be invariant. I believe that this interpretation is also the key to a true evaluation of the so-called post-conciliar reneval in theology. None of the trends of renewal should be absolutized; they are only new "languages of coordinates". For that reason it is good that there are many of them, good - under the condition that none of them will contain anachronistic elements taken from an already outdated picture of the world.

One can also state more briefly: the Truth of Faith is too transcendental to be enclosed in one theological system. The more systems, the better the chance that one can grasp something of this Truth. Although "Invariant", Truth is multi-aspected and one can view it through many prisms.

25

Two:

Antinomies of Co-existence

1. Content and Attitude.

In examining the development of relations between faith and science in modern times, one can perceive a clear shift in accent. At first certain scientific assertions seemed to contradict religious truths. This set up and then intensified the problem. In time the "differences in opinion" of science and faith become less important, while an ever grater role began to be played by the difference in mentalities. This led to a difference of two planes in the entire dispute: the plane of content and the plane of attitude. The dispute remained on the plane of content, but more and more rises to the plane of attitude.

The intensity of the debate on the plane of content has clearly lessened. Perhaps each person experiencing the problem of science and faith must pass through this stage, and for this reason problems of content continually reappear in discussions with high school students and in those circles in which the nineteenth century interpretation of science encounters the medieval conception of faith. But among more tenacious theologians there is, rather, a general opinion that the problems of content in the dispute of science and faith have been basically solved, while the essential problem today is the plane of attitude.

The solution of problems of content was achieved by two methods: division and purification (1). The separation of religious from scientific cognition by type: both of these kinds of cognition differ as to their epistemology, methods, and language. All of this assigns to them separate areas of competency, in principle not having a common part. The process of the purification ("demythologization") of theology from pseudo-scientific and pseudo-dogmatic elements (see the previous chapter) removed many of the substantial contradictions between science and faith and showed how such contradictions should be removed in the future.

The process of separation has gone so far that many theologians believe that real conflicts of content between science and faith cannot exist at all, since science and faith belong to complete separate, mutually untranslatable cognitive plans.

This kind of evolution of theology (and theologians) became possible because of an evolution within science. Science today has reached a high degree of maturity, has created reflections on itself (philosophy of science), discovered the limits of its method and assumptions, on which the use of these methods is tacitly based. This gave theologians an instrument for making separating distinctions.

In any case, it is a fact that despite longings for The Great Synthesis today's "vision of the world" is undergoing stratification. One assumes - as Ladriere says - a certain discontinuity of experience. The stratification of systems is not synthesis, but it does make symbiosis possible.

There remains the difference in attitudes. This is not only a psychological problem - that different mentalities give rise to the feeling of mutual strangeness or animosity, but also a problem in the philosophy of knowledge - to what extent do attitudes or mentality reflect real differences or cognitive levels.

Moving the focal point of the problem science-faith from the plane of content to the plane of attitude means passage from discussion of specific questions to posing the problem in a more general, but also more fundamental, way. Advances in the philosophy of science have made it possible to speak of science as a whole, considering not the encyclopedic listing of its results but its epistemological and methodological functions.

In the presently developing phase of the problem science-faith the strangeness of attitudes has taken the place of conflict. The following parts of this chapter are devoted to an analysis of what this strangeness is.

2. Temptation of Empiricism.

One of the most fundamental sources of the strangeness of the scientific attitude in relation to the attitude of faith is certainly the empiricism of modern science. It is no exaggeration to state that the empirical method is incontestably the greatest success of post-Newtonian science. One's relation to this method determines the so-called scientific mentality. Quite commonly it is imputed that the "scientific mentality" reduces its whole philosophy to the slogan: "I believe in nothing that I cannot touch and measure". One can agree with this only under the condition that this slogan is understood very symbolically. The empiricism of modern science is at least in equal measure a "pane and eye" and exactness of thought. The connection between experience and mathematized speculation is compulsory at all stages of scientific research: from the preliminary collection of empirical data, through the most far-reaching formal generalization, up to the observational testing of specific results deduced mathematically from the accepted assumptions. Mathematical deduction is just as compellingly obvious to the mind as experience is to the senses. The mind sees the necessity of mathematical connections just as the eye sees the readings of some measuring instrument.

This "obviousness" of the scientific method is strengthened still further by its extraordinary effectiveness. From the time that empirics and mathematics solidified their position in the investigation of the world, science ceased to serve only the erudition of scholars and became an instrument for subordinating nature to human purposes. Nature submits to man only when he commands it through the language of mathematized empirics. The development of technology is a natural consequence of mathematical-empirical way of looking at nature.

The totalitarian tendencies of modern science stem from these premises. If these mathematical-experimental methods are so obviously successful, then do any other methods of studying reality exist - and are they at all necessary? Various kinds of reductionism began with a negative answer to this question; among them particularly physicalism - the program of reducing all of science to physics, or, what practically amounts to the same thing, the program of extending the method used by physics to all sciences; and reductionism understood as a catchword for reducing all philosophy to the methodology of sciences. It is a fact that none of these reductionisms has been achievable to date (which certainly, by itself, is still not evidence that they cannot be achieved). They remain only more or less supported catchwords and programs.

The essence of totalism is that one can speak of a certain kind of psychological pressure to agree to reductionist programs. This pressure is all the stronger the more elusive it is. It is not brought about by any scientific institution, but by mechanisms of the psyche of a person who in life practice has encountered the methods of science, above all a person who uses these methods daily in a certain scientific field. I believe that a true understanding of the empirical attitude excludes totalisms. Totalism is always pressure a priori, and empiricism opposes apriorism. Empiricism enjoins one to test, experiment and not to agree beforehand to the regime of untested programs.

Sound reductionism can be very useful: when methods which have proven successful in one field are tried out in another. For this gives the hope of progress. But reductionism can be sound only when one does not discriminate in advance other methods, which have already proven themselves in other areas of reality.

Empirical totalism willingly uses the catchword of Wittgenstein: "What we cannot speak about we must pass over in silence". But we know that situations exist in which silence is consent to certain contents, and lack of choice - choice. And most often the worst choice possible.

3. The Anthropological Revolution.

Another of its extremely attractive features results from the empiricism of the scientific method - objectivism. And hence, not "as it seems to me", but "as it really is". Idealism (epistemological) and realism, Descartes and Kant, Husserl's science without assumptions and positivistic debates on the meaning of language - are only often too feverish and not always successful attempts to overcome that "which seems to me" in order to reach that "which is".

Philosophy is ever more aware that it cannot transcend the human frame of reference. To acquiesce to something that is unavoidable anyway facilitates, and sometimes simply makes possible survival. Perhaps it was Kierkegaard who was the first to venture the statement that "objective truth" is not important, even if it were possible to attain. What is important is my own, subjective existence; how I see reality becomes a part of myself. This point of view was favored by philosophers of the twentieth century, except that the word "subjectivism" (despite all weighed down with negative connotations) is replaced with the term "anthropologism". Philosophy is to be anthropological, which means that it is not only to defend the interests of man, but above all is to share with man his privileges and limitations, it is to be a human way of looking at reality.

The "return to man" in philosophy could not remain without influence on modern theological formulations. There is no lack of voices that all of dogmatic theology should become theological anthropology.

"If one wishes to treat all of dogmatics as transcendental anthropology, then in relation to everything of which dogmatics speaks one must ask about the neseccary conditions of cognition in the subject, in the theologian. This operation will indicate the existence of a priori conditions of cognition in the subject, and also that these conditions assume and say something about this subject and determine the manner, method, and limits of his cognition. ... And discovery of this connection between the content of dogmatic pronouncements and human experience of oneself is nothing else but the application of the anthropological and transcendental method in theology." (2)

Even without the anthropological revolution theology was charged with extreme subjectivism. Religious faith is one of the most intimate experiences of man, amd it is very easy to equate this intimacy - falsely - with subjectivism.

It is precisely here that the contrast with the empirical method appears: the abstractness of religion - the concreteness of scientific experience, the unverifiability of theological assertions - the compulsion of empiricism, the privateness of faith - the intersubjectiveness of science.

Indeed, for the broad masses (including here very many scientists) objectivity is synonymous with science, and objectivity determines the tremendous authority which science enjoys today. But if we wish to go beyond current formulations, it turns out that the problem of the objectivity of scientific cognition is not so simple and requires deeper reflection.

4. The Principle of Objectivity.

Scientists often speak of the principle of objectivity, compulsory in scientific cognition. According to Whitehead, "nature can be thought of as a closed system whose

31

mutual relations do not require the expression of the fact that they are thought about". Such thinking about nature is objective thinking ("homogeneous" in Whitehead's terminology) (3). The principle of objectivity operates most strongly in the area of physical sciences. Schroedinger also calls this principle the "hypothesis of the real world". It consists in that that "we exclude the Subject of Cognizance from the domain of nature that we endeavour to understand. ... a moderately satisfying picture of the world has only been reached at the high price of taking ourselves out of the picture, stepping back into the role of a non-concerned observer." (4)

Some believe that after the appearance of quantum mechanics - one of whose co-creators was Schroedinger - the situation changed. The very act of measuring a microphysical system (e.g. an elementary particle) introduces significant disturbances within this system. It is impossible to draw a sharp boundary line between the investigating observer and the investigated object. The subject becomes part of the investigated reality. Anti-objectivistic tendencies suggested by quantum mechanics are more and more definitely gaining a place in the philosophy of science. Now even in textbook formulations it is stated that it is "the scientist who creates order", and that "the biological evolution is the only process we know of through which order can arise from disorder, i.e. through which one can create information".

One could certainly write an extensive treatise on the principle of objectivity in the empirical sciences. Without doubt many formulations and shades of meaning of this principle could be distinguished. It is also probable that neither too strong nor too weak formulations are valid in present-day science, and if we wish to be objective, we should recognize the "human component" in the product of our own scientific activity. This component is much smaller in the empirical sciences than in any of the other fields of cognition.

5. An Elusive Boundary.

After the previous - of necessity quite abbreviated - analyses, we get the impression that the difference between scientific and religious cognition is somehow obliterated. It certainly exists, but it is more of a "continuum" than it seemed to the previous generation of philosophers of science. In general outline we say: empiricism, hence verifiability, and thus objectivity - on the side of science; non-empiricism, lack of verifiability, subjectivism - on the side of faith. But when we delve more deeply into the problem, it turns out that a strict understanding of empiricism (as with the neopositivists) resolves itself into the construction of science exclusively from material supplied by the senses, and hence at bottom to a purely subjective factor. The postulate of verifiability in the modern philosophy of science is more and more yielding place to a pragmatism which cannot be more precisely defined. The anthropological tendencies of modern theology are clearly striving for its objectification, while the tendency to retain objectivism in the empirical sciences leads directly to awareness of the anthropological element at the foundation of these sciences. The sternness of empirics stands opposed to methodological totalism, while the critical attitude, which is also compulsory toward empirics, in experimental practice forces us to perceive elements of belief in another person, and hence elements of faith.

For documentary evidence of the departure of the philosophy of science from naive empiricism we recall the opinion of Quine that the entities which physics speaks of differ from the gods of Homer only in their degree of usefulness (5).

Despite the fact that - as it turns out - the differences between the "attitude of science" and the "attitude of faith" cannot be simply highlighted, the strangeness of these attitudes in some sense quite intrusive, and even continually sharpened by various "external factors" (i.e. those not resulting directly from theories of scientific and religious cognition), such as: the continually accumulating history of the problem, disputes which, even if they are resolved, leave permanent traces on the social subconscious, environmental pressures, psychological conditioning, etc. These external irritations are so closely bound up with the essence of the problem that it is impossible to make any unequivocal distinctions here. If distinctions are impossible, it also means that they are superfluous. One must face the problem in its overall complications.

6. Strangeness.

And in general outline the problem is as follows. science - whatever it might be, more or less empirical, objectivistic or anthropologial - is solely a work of man. In the sense that man himself, with the help of methods discovered by himself, acquires information (even if it belonged completely to the external world and said nothing about him), he orders, digests, and tests it. Science is the product of man's activity. On the other hand, faith in the religious sense is by definition acceptance of a "voice from beyond". The rational activity of man here only consists in applying certain criteria to this voice, on evaluating the degree of its credibility. The rest is acceptance, answer, ex post reflection on the content of the "order from superior authority" (so theology comes into being), an effort to base one's life on it.

The essence of the strangeness of the "attitude of science" and the "attitude of faith" is that the former comes "from the Earth", the latter – "from Heaven". This is the source of both methodological distinctions as well as all psychological resistance

Psychologically speaking, the first and essential conflict between science and faith stems from the fact that a mind trained in methods of scientific cognition, and thus in the independent, human investigation of reality, hesitates to accept "information from the outside". God, who not only should exist – man himself can still understand this – but who also has spoken to us is a "foreign body" for our knowledge, is precisely "information from above".

More recent theological formulations have tried to mitigate this strangeness, treating Revelation not so much as "information from above", but, rather, as a personal, existential dialogue of man with the Revealing One. This formulation is certainly more valid from a theological point of view, but in no way does it alter the strangeness which we are discussing. Every dialogue is alike in that it is That Other One who speaks.

The strangeness of the attitudes of science and faith is fundamental and cannot be eliminated by any measures. And, I would even say, authentic faith requires the continual sharpening of this strangeness. Faith, after all, is trust in the Other One.

7. Marginal, but Important, Conclusions.

The conflict between science and faith on some one of its lower levels is certainly connected with the manner in which the principles of faith are transmitted and certainly could be significantly mitigated were this transmission to take a form more adapted to what we call the scientific mentality.

The scientific mentality, or simply the mentality of scientists (especially those to whom methodological reflection on their own activity is not alien), is accustomed to recognize assertions and scientific theories with their entire ballast of various assumptions and limitations. The necessity for basing oneself on assumptions, a whole system of limitations, and hence a certain relativity of acquired information, are inseparable features of human cognition. The believer must certainly accept that in his religion there is something which can be called the eternal, unchanging current of Truth. I fear that too often religion is preached as a set of ultimate, categorical formulas. Even if this is only a superficial impression, resulting from the fact that the preacher uses mental abbreviations or terminology, which mean something in his language, but not much in the language of the listener, even still it is a dangerous phenomenon. One cannot forget that for many people "from outside" or "from the borderline" contact with religion is often superficial.

The result of scientific activity is regarded as a certain collection of information, and for that reason the scientist-believer is strongly tempted to regard a religious transmission as new information, only that was not acquired by his own powers. Also favoring this view is the preaching of religion, though still not so frequently, on the model of some sort of system of knowledge of the world. It is hardly surprising that for those who (correctly) feel that for the investigation of the world human knowledge, though imperfect, is completely adequate religious faith is difficult to open their doors to.

In this context, I regard a certain anthropologism of revelation, stressed by modern theology, as especially valuable and worth popularizing in methods of preaching faith. Religious truths, even though they might contain certain assertions about the world (e.g. the truth about the creation of the world), are at bottom truths for man and about man and were transmitted to us as such. They are not supposed to suggest to us knowledge about the world, which we can and should acquire by ourselves; their purpose is always to reveal to man truth about himself, his relation to God, his way to the Absolute Reality. This knowledge - or, better perhaps, skill, for without putting it into practice it remains empty - is necessary to every man. And to the creators of science as well.

And, above all, the Word on the Truth should be transmitted with humility, and not with the feeling of a participant in God's omniscience. It is worth reminding oneself and those to whom one preaches (and everyone who believes in a certain sense simultaneously preaches) that in speaking of truth we use a certain model (arrangement of concepts, language) which was created by the process of the development of our culture. A good analogy is physical reality and its scientific description. We believe that our description represents reality, but we know that it is more scanty. How much more scanty must be a model in which we transmit religious truth from Truths itself.

Only humble preaching in the belief that we are given to understand little and only within a conceptual model accessible solely to our culture can bring the Word closer to those for whom it would be difficult to accept that knowledge of the relation of man to God was given to us in an easy and finished manner, whereas knowledge of the Universe is acquired with such great effort.

Three:

Antinomies of Action

1. From the Head of a Wise Man.

On the inside of the cover of "Summa Technologica" by
Stanislaw Lem (I have before me the edition of 1967, Cracow)
there appears a drawing - the geneology of man: a powerful
tree growing out of the ground by various amoebae and
starfish; the main trunk leads through fishes, reptiles,
amphibians and in a certain place branches off: a strong side
branch gives off insects and ends - almost blindly - in small,
too highly specialized new growths; the main trunk of the tree
bends dangerously to one side, but - a little against the laws
of equilibrium - does not break but laboriously climbs upward,
generating ever more simian-like, then ever more humanoid
forms; this did not happen without discards: many
side-branches ending without leaves or suddenly broken off; on
the swaying tip of the already too slender main trunk sits
Homo Sapiens, holding a fragile branch with all his might;
equilibrium is still further impaired by a strange new
construction growing out of the head of the Wise Man: this is
the further extension of the tree, but the bark has been
replaced by metal and the knots and grains - by screws and
wires; the first product generated by vital fluids of the
human brain, grafted onto the already sligtly decaying baobab
of life, is a calculating machine, followed by successive
generations of computers, various ENIACs, UNIVACs, MANIACs
(!!!); evolution becomes entangled in a thicket of loops and
branches, only on one, completely side-branch a small spring
juts out pointing toward the future...

37

Technology is not a simple, linear extension of biological evolution. From the point of view of physics organic life reduces itself to routine processes, or to a specific construction, and so from the very beginning there is something in the way of a technical operation (though not understood mechanically). The degree of arrangement can be measured. As is known, the measure of arrangement is a function called entropy: a lesser entropy corresponds to a higher order, greater entropy – to a lesser order. In the non-organic world, "made up" almost exclusively of irreversible processes, there is a general tendency toward the growth of entropy (the second law of thermodynamics), the non-organic world tends toward disorganization. In the animate world, on the contrary, both the evolution of life as a whole as well as the development of the single organism lead to the lessening of entropy or to the growth of organization. Of course, this does not occur contrary to the laws of physics. Life – according to the well-known statement of Schroedinger – feeds on negative entropy. The consumption of reserves depletes the supply in the cupboard. Local lessening of entropy in animate forms takes place at the cost of a more rapid growth of entropy in the supersystem, of which the living organism is a subsystem. The total balance sheet even so gives a general growth of entropy. In this light optimistic visions stating that the processes of evolution will someday overcome processes of dissipation are pure utopia.

Man imitates nature in its evolutionary strategy. The entire technical activity of man at bottom consists in "organizing" nature, in creating a "new order", and is thus a process leading in the direction of lessening entropy. Technology is man's game with nature; in this case the game must be played between the inexorable, universal trend toward the growth of entropy and the maximum utilization of the possibility of its local (in time and space) lessening.

The test of strength between man and nature changes into a conscious game from the time when the empirical sciences began to reveal the rules of the game. Prior to that there was no game, only a riddle. Today it is difficult to draw an unequivocal boundary between science and technology. Science has become more technological, technology, more scientific. The effectiveness of scientific methods appears not only in the accurate forecasting of the results of future experiments, but also – and for many people, above all – in technical applications. It is essentially through the mediation of technology that science interferes in our daily

life. And for that reason the "technological mentality" today
is more universal phenomenon than the "scientific mentality".
In the remainder of this chapter I wish to consider
some of the relations between the technological mentality and
the problem of religious faith. I shall not attempt a more
global formulation - library shelves are bursting with various
analyses of the problem of technology - I shall only attempt
to formulate the thoughts which are on my mind.

2. Triumph and Alarm.

The essence of the problem seems apparent. In a
natural way I divide the world surrounding me into two
regions: that which I can act upon and make use of for my own
purposes and everything that I do not know, against which I am
powerless, and what - I feel this to be so - exerts pressure
on me. In the consciousness of "pre-technological" peoples
this division was very sharp: the region under control was the
sphere of secularity, the independent region was sacrum. Since
the secular sphere encompassed only the region within the
reach of the two hands, nearly everything was subject to
religious authority, and various practices in the form of
cults attempted to replace the technological means of acting
on nature. With the development of science and its
technological applications the proportions between such an
understanding of secularity and sacredness drastically
changed. The secular sphere expanded enormously and today
encompasses the entire visible horizon. Of course, there are
still very many unresolved questions (the chain reaction of
problems: one resolved problem poses dozens of new problems):
a tremendous amount of the "forces of nature" eludes human
control, but modern man firmly believes that in principle all
of them can be subjected to the methods worked out by science.
The world has become secularized, and there is no place in it
for sacrum. Religion seems superfluous, and the measures which
it suggests, naively ineffective in man's contact with nature.
Broadly speaking, the atheism of the technological era
takes two forms. The first is "triumphant atheism": the
triumph of a man who thinks that through technological
manipulations he has achieved complete power over nature. God
for him has become an "unnecessary hypothesis". The second
form of atheism we call after Rahner "alarmed atheism":
"horrified by the absence of God in the world, the feeling
that divinity has become fictitious, confusion through the
silence of God, His confinement in His own inaccessibility, the

39

lack of meaning in the growing secularization of the world, the blindness and anonimity of its laws" (1).

These forms of strangeness, aversion, or animosity (they reach various degrees of intensity) toward religion are in some sense vulgarized forms of positivistic metaphysics: God is unnecessary, for He does not materialize in experience as understood in one way or another.

3. The New Man.

We often observe extreme attitudes toward technological progress. In the development of technology some perceive the source of all evil, others see in it the panaceum for all human ills. Pessimism in its darkest version simply foresees the destruction of our planet and therewith the automatic solution of all conflicts. (This reminds me of certain moralist, who, among the causes eliminating passion, mentioned "the biological death of the subject of passion".) Optimism occasions the creation of a New Man, Technological Man, who certainly now is more of a myth than reality, but who, when he appears will be a man controlling his own development, will represent a new type of culture, which will prove to be the intellectual leaven for all of the leading strata of the society. The only salvation for the race is the creation of technological man.

These statements come from the book "Technological Man: the Myth and the Reality" by V. G. Ferkiss (2). It is worth examining somewhat more closely the profile of Technological Man as seen through the eyes of this author.

Above all - in Ferkiss' opinion - Technological Man will control the technology which he has created. If there is command and control, then in whose interest and in accordance with what norms? And so Technological Man must have a certain philosophy. What kind of philosophy will this be? Ferkiss mentions three basic elements: new naturalism, new holism, and new immanentism.

Naturalism: man in reality is rather a part of nature than something separated from it; the Universe in a certain sense is an equilibrium in constant movement, an equilibrium of which man is an inseparable part. Holism: the fundamental concepts of development assume that no part can be defined or understood otherwise than in connection with the whole. Immanentism: this whole - both cosmic as well as social - is a new kind of whole, determined not from outside, but from within.

This "three-point" philosophy is to assure Technological Man an ideology with which he can effectively face the "existential revolution", which is a necessary consequence of the technological revolution. For every individual and every society the key problem is the problem of freedom. Man cannot attain freedom by standing on the sidelines. The actions of others influence him - he is thus an object of "power", but he also "rules", for he acts on the others. The whole is present in all its parts.

The consciousness of freedom requires an ethic. This will be an ethic completely grounded in the place of man in the whole. Here are some of the "ethical laws" proposed by Ferkiss: man should not engage in the conquest of nature, but coexist with it in harmony; man must maintain a distinction between himself and the machines which he has created, man's becoming dependent on components of the whole of a lower order, such as machines, would be anti-evolutionary behavior; man should also control his own evolution, etc.

The technical revolution and the existential revolution, taking place on the canvas of general development, must also create a new culture. New naturalism, new holism, and new immanentism should be predominant and inspiring subjects to the same extent as were the world views of medieval Christianty and bourgeois mechanistic materialism in earlier epochs. Teaching and education, art, relations between the sexes and generations, literature, philosophy and religion - all these elements of culture must reflect the new world view not only in a clear and apparent manner, but also in the categories of their own internal processes and styles.

The picture sketched by Ferkiss is striking in its naivete. The "three-point" philosophy today is a metaphysics often repeated in different versions, nota bene not having much in common with the real results of the empirical sciences; furthermore, panevolutionism extended to the Universe (Ferkiss in many places professes just such a view), as we have seen, is quite clearly in conflict with the presently accepted principles of physics.

The human inner world cannot be manipulated through ordinary technological operations. And it is precisely man's inner self that must be changed if man is not to become a slave to machines and technology. And for that reason he creates ideologies. An ideology is good if it stresses its scientific character as often as necessary and if it is made up of enough commonplaces so as to attract the largest number of people without the difficulty of delving into its contents. And it is precisely in this that efforts to manipulate society through technology consist. The reformatory spirit fills the pages written by Ferkiss, but all reforms undertaken in the name of catchwords dreamed up behind a desk either remain harmless literature or change into just such a technology of managing social groups, not always for worthy ends. Besides, the views of Ferkiss presented here should not be taken too seriously; they were selected rather at random. Their significance lies, at most, in their typicalness.

4. A Deeper Dimension of Holiness.

In the context of similar views, at least in the feeling of a large number of people, there is no place for God. It is just at this point that alarmed or triumphant atheism arises, depending on the psychological and philosophical disposition of the given person.

Are these atheisms really experience of the "death of God"? For many people it is certainly so, but in this process one can also discern a certain form of maturation of the religious consciousness of contemporary man. In what sense? The development of science set in motion, and then accelerated, the process of the demythologization of ideas about God and His activity (see chapter 1). This process occured mainly among scientists and theologians. Technical progress overturns the artificial division of the world into a secular sphere under technical control and an inaccessible sacrum. This progress goes on in the broad circles of the society and is, as it were, a popularized - and of necessity also vulgarized - form of the previous process. Atheisms of the technological era for some are experience of the death of God, and for others, experience of the death - in painful and decidedly too long agony - of the former established pattern of the world.

A world divided into spheres of man's and God's influence is not in keeping with the Christian doctrine. Such a picture was tempting for less discriminating theologians, who from the gap in human science attempted to formulate proofs for the existence of God. In accordance with views which have their roots in the philosophy of Aristotle, God was treated as the First Cause. It is hardly surprising, then, that if science had no ready explanations for some phenomenon or class of phenomena, some theologians - using their language - supplemented the absence of secondary causes with the direct action of the First Cause.

Contemporary theology carefully avoids such kinds of operations. Theologians have even modified their terminology. They more willingly speak of categorial causes and the Transcendental Cause (God) than of secondary causes and the First Cause. The Transcendental Cause (God) is not a cause acting "alongside" other causes, nor does it in any way supplement the inadequacy or weakness of categorial causes (formerly: secondary causes). The Transcendental Cause works in all other causes, it is due to it that all other causes can be causes at all, it inheres in their activity. Therefore, it is fruitless to search in the world for some "traces" of God, from which we could make inference about the existence of the First Cause. Every effect is exclusively the work of ordinary causes (categorial). It is the task of science to reconstruct the sequence of these causes and science will never go outside of this sequence. This is so-called natural explanation. Thus, for example, the biological sciences are to reconstruct the sequel of successive natural causes (categorial) which led to the origin of life. It would be an unscientific operation to utilize the gap in this sequence still not filled in by scientific theory and fill it with the statement that the first living cell was created through the remarkable intervention of God in the course of evolution.

But every effect is also exclusively the work of the Transcendental Cause. If it were not for this cause, other causes would not exist at all. There are no "traces of God" in the world, for the whole of reality is one such great trace. "The world became - Rahner writes - a dimension closed within itself, and not, as it were, open in some places with God passing through them, nor experiencing in some places possible to observe 'divine pushes'. Only as a whole and in a very inconscious manner does it point to God as to its a priori." (3)

The language of causes is alien to the modern experimental science. For that reason the entire above argument about categorial causes and the Transcendental Cause still sounds strange to someone familiar with the empirical sciences. However, beyond these formulations let us attempt to extract the content. The thoughts which I have attempted to present are well summarized by a statement from an ascetic booklet: Sacrum in Christianity is a deeper dimension of a Whole, and not another part of life.

5. Still More on Naturalism, Holism, and Immanentism.

And so what contents are hidden within the new theological formulations presented above? Above all, they respect the autonomy of scientific explanation, it is natural explanation. God - the Transcendental Cause exists in the world, but not as remarkable "pushes" given to nature, but through His natural activity; this activity manifests in the existence of what is. This doctrine can be called the Christian version of naturalism. Since we recogize God through His activity, we should seek him in the world and in ourselves. This is Christian immanentism. But - we remember - in nature there are no individual "traces" of God. Only the world as a whole points to its a priori. Hence there is also Christian holism.

Christian naturalism, immanentism, and holism are not only a doctrine about God, but also about man. Man, after all, is the main partner of what determines unity, wholeness, consanguinuity.

We see that today's Christian thought is tormented by the same tendencies as is Technological Man.

The consequence of the naturalistic, holistic, and immanent treatment of man is his technological task of reshaping reality to his needs and purposes. Just at this point the extraordinary effectiveness of technical action contrasts with the helplessness of religion. I am inclined to regard such charges as a plain misunderstanding, or even the incomprehension of religion. Behavior which is the organic component of genuine religiosity is one of the most difficult, but also one of the most authentic forms of behavior. This is no longer the subjection of external matter to treatment; here it is a question of transforming one's self, one's own personality. Technological progress without moral development would result in the gradual enslavement of man to social mechanisms. Technological Man lacking an effective ethic would be a cripple - though perhaps in certain fields an efficient - robot. Religion supplies such an ethic.

6. Tools and Language.

Tools are connected with the energetic aspect of man's game with nature, language - with informational problems. Without tools and language technology could not have come into being and developed. Tools make possible man's deeper, not merely superficial, interference in the course of nature;

language is the fundamental mean enabling people to communicate with each other and to store acquired information. The dependencies between tools and language go even further. At the beginning of this chapter I said that the whole of man's technical activity reduces itself to "arranging" nature, thus in the light of information theory it is the production of information (4). According to some modern philsophical formulations, the "substance" of the Universe is not only mass-energy, but also information. A certain amount of information is coded within the structure of nature; science deals with its de-coding. Each discovered law of nature is information which we have been able to read. In this context the technical activity of man takes on new meaning. Through technical activity man creatively joins in the creation of information. Tools and language unite. We produce meanings which we must then understand.

Recapitulation

Human thought measuring itself against Revealed Truth
is the source of Christian theology. From it theology also
draws the power for its continual progress.

In the development of mutual conflicts between human
thought and Revelation one can distinguish certain phases.

The first phase is setting the stage of the conflict:
Revealed Truth had to express itself in the language
available, created by Judeo-Graeco-Roman culture. And it
immediately burst the conceptual framework of this language.
It could not have been otherwise. There must exist an enormous
lack of proportion between revealed content and the means of
expression available to people. Setting the stage of the
conflict took place in Christian antiquity.

With time, more or less loose reflection on Revelation
was organized into theology. The search for truths "without the
aid of Revelation" became the domain of philosophy. The
dispute over competencies between theology and philosophy is
the significance of the entire history of medieval thought. We
observe the systematic   growth of "theological scepticism":
philosophy abandons an ever greater number of its theses,
transferring them to theology. Metaphorically, ever less is
proved, ever more is believed in. The process of the
separation of faith from knowledge began long before the
sciences came into being. This was the second phase of the
conflict.

The origin of the empirical sciences initiated the
third phase. Philosophy and theology were too highly
specialized in their scholastic evolution to be able to adapt

to the changed conditions. Isolating self-defense mechanisms were set in motion. Their working continues - and even deepens - to this day. Efforts to cross the isolating barrier primarily had the character of "short clashes". The "case of Copernicus" and the "case of Darwin" are most typical examples and, as it were, symbols of the entire dispute. We usually have this stage of the conflict in mind when we speak of the conflict science-faith.

In the long process of development, human thought strengthened and became more critical in relation to itself. Theology owes much to the clash with maturing human thought, above all the process of purifying it from "pseudo-dogmas". By pseudo-dogmas one should here understand certain elements of the picture of the world created by the science of a former epoch, which so fused with the form of Revelation that they were erroneously taken as revealed contents. The development of science demythologized many of these elements and taught us to be careful about this in the future.

Because of this we have become more clearly aware than ever before that Revealed Truth is an "Invariant" to which we never have direct access; we can only ineffectively express it in the language of various "coordinate frames".

The history of the problem teaches us a lesson. And what is the present state of the conflict? The dispute remained on the level of content: certain assertions of science seemed to contradict certain religious truths; today the conflict is taking place on the level of attitude: the scientific attitude does not seem to leave room for religious belief.

The differences between the "mentality of science" and the "mentality of faith" cannot be clearly delineated. Closer examination reveals a continuum rather than sharp boundaries. For example, the rigorous empiricism of science is easily reduced to the tendency to base everything on sense impressions, and thus at bottom on a subjective factor. On the other hand, anthropological formulations of modern theology clearly strive toward its objectivization. In turn, the desire to retain objectivity in the empirical sciences leads to an awareness of the anthropological element at the base of these sciences.

Notwithstanding, the feeling of the strangeness of science in relation to faith is highly conspicuous. The essence of the "strangeness" consists in the fact that science is exclusively the product of man's activity, while religious faith is acceptance of the Word. Even if acceptance of the Word is understood not as the recording of information from above, but as a personal dialogue, it is always a going outside the sphere of one's own, exclusively human activity and opening oneself to the One-Who-Speaks-the-Word.

The authenticity of faith requires the continual sharpening of this "strangeness". Any effort to obliterate it whatsoever would lead to a falsification of the essence of religious experience.

Very often the feeling of strangeness occuring between faith and knowledge takes on a vulgarized form: science, thanks to its extension - technology, is characterized by unusual effectiveness in transforming the world; in comparison with it religion seems weak and powerless.

The sphere of reality which man controls through his technological possibilities becomes something familiar, (secular) to him. The sphere which eludes technical control he is inclined to regard as sacrum. Since the man of today - at least in his ambitions - controls everything, sacrum for him shrinks to zero.

A world divided into spheres under man's and God's influence is inconsistent with Christian doctrine. Sacrum is a deeper dimension of a Whole, and not a subregion isolated from the domain of ordinary human activity. Sacrum also reaches into the very depths of man himself. Authentic religion must be effective in action. Except that here one is not concerned with the transformation of external matter, but, rather, the transformation of one's own self. Technological development without moral development would result in man's enslavement to social mechanisms. Technological man without an effective ethic would become a non-human robot.

2

SECOND HAND

Second hand - since this part contains a discussion of several readings which helped me in my considerations. Thus I am presenting the views of others, but not in the form of a simple report; these are rather thoughts jotted down on the margins of the books which I have read.

I admit that these books were selected rather at random. They are simply the ones which I encountered, and since they interested me, I read them carefully. Despite this, however, this set of readings which gave rise to these chapters forms a certain logical whole.

In the first part I tried to grasp the meaning of the problem "science and faith" in its most general, historical, and contemporary framework. In this, the second part I am attempting to deepen these considerations by a more detailed examination of several more specific problems.

And so in chapters four and five I focus on two critical points in the history of the relations between science and faith. The first reading (chapter 4) takes a closer look at the period of the "mechanistic revolution" when the nascent and actively developing sciences (more or less in the seventeenth-eighteenth centuries) formed in human minds a new picture of the world, based almost exclusively on Newton's mechanics. The second reading (chapter 5) centers on a period in which - after the many upheavals which took place in science at the beginning of the twentieth century - a neopositivistic type of philosophy became dominant, undermining the reasonableness of any problems whatever outside a narrowly defined scientific empiricism.

The next two readings (written from positions hostile to religion) concern two specific issues full of internal tension and misunderstandings of long account. The first issue consists of theological implications of the evolution of the Universe, especially of its beginning (chapter 6); the second, those of the evolution of life, especially of its origin.

Four:

Looking at Earlier Disputes through Modern Eyes

1. Introduction.

The changes essential for our culture which occured in the period from the beginning of modern times up to the nineteenth century inclusively are something more than history. In the course of reading, a by no means simple picture gradually emerges from the specialized studies and polemics between experts. Its details become rearranged, change their hues, until finally, toward the end, they form a whole which though cluttered with details, is synthetic enough to produce a general view.

Before me is a book – an anthology of historical studies – devoted, as the editor writes, to the mutual interactions between science and religious beliefs (1). This book is distinguished by its clearly English character. The dispute science-faith in modern times enveloped the whole compass of so-called Western culture, but this time as well the British Isles were characteristic in their individuality. If one considers that both Newton and Darwin – two names marking successive phases of the dispute – were Englishmen, then the English accents here can be highly interesting.

2. Atomism and Moses.

For a man from the Continent the modern science-faith dispute begins with Galileo, for the Englishman with the problem of atomism. This can be seen in the growth of publications in England in the second half of the seventeenth century devoted to Epicurus. Some authors (Lasawitz) regard Daniel Sennert as the creator of naturalistic atomism, born 1572 in Silesia and later associated with the University of Wittenburg. In one of his writings ("Hypomnematum Physicorum", 1636) he presented something like a history of atomism; there we find a brief note that atomistic views were already professed by "one Mochus a Phoenician, who is reputed to have flourished before the destruction of Troy". This statement supplied the apologists with a weapon.

It was then widely held that atomism leads to materialistic views. Of course, this position elicited a reaction. There were two tactics of counterargumentation. The first stemmed from the assumptions of atomism itself: since atoms are characterized by inertia, there must exist a non-material factor which set them in motion. The second tactic, more characteristic of that time, referred to the history of the problem by attempting to show that atomism has its roots not in atheistic Greek philosophy but in biblical tradition. The first tactic later bore fruit in the philosophy of Newton, the second created the so-called Mosaic philosophy (Philosophia Mosaica), work of the Renaissance, which departed from the historical stage along with the Renaissance itself.

Sennert's comment was a good opportunity. All one had to do was to identify Mochus the Phoenician with the biblical Moses. And this was in keeping with earlier tendencies. Marsilio Ficino already had not only emphasized the parallelism between Platonism and Mosaism, but believed that certain elements of Hebrew tradition had entered into Hellenistic culture. Later similar views were expressed on many occasions.

We shall not follow D. B. Sailor (2) in the detailed history of these rather strange views. It is only worth noting that traces of the "Mosaic philosophy" can be found in the writings of scientists of such stature as Boyle and Newton. Boyle as well as Newton maintained rather close contacts with the Cambridge Platonists, and though the writings of both show that they were aware of the problems connected with the parallels between the works of the Greek philosophers and the

Bible, neither Boyle nor Newton drew any conclusions from this fact.

We might add that the eventual conflict between atomism and religious assertions in the seventeenth century could not be, in the strict meaning of the word, a conflict between science and religion, because atomism did not become a full-fledged scientific theory until the nineteenth century. Seventeenth century atomism was partly a scientific speculation and partly a philosophical doctrine, only more compatible with the spirit of Newton's mechanics than was the earlier conception of matter which went back to Aristotle.

3. Christian Doctrine and Appearance of the Sciences.

Herbert Butterfield did not hesitate to state that the appearance of the sciences "outshines everything since the rise of Christianity" (3). If the modern sciences are not to be regarded as the product of some sort of collective intellectual mutation, then the appearance of these sciences must be examined within the entire context of the cultural tradition. Only twentieth century studies on the history of science (Duhem, Sudhoff, Little, Sarton, Haskins, Thorndike) appreciated the role of the Middle Ages in preparing the scientific revolution which took place at the beginning of modern times. Even upheavals do not sever a certain continuity of scientific development. A. R. Hall (4) believes that the main factor in the progress of science is the "internal dynamics" within science itself. Explanations for transformations of the intellect should be sought in the history of intellect. External factors - social, economic, for example - play only a secondary role here. Sociology of science without the philosophy of science is unable to explain why science develops.

The internal logic of the development of science leads us to seek out the previous links of the chain of evolution in the history of the intellect, but there one must discover those factors which make the next links something really new in comparison with the old ones. The editor of the book under discussion as a classical example of this cites the study of M. B. Foster (5). Let us pause to consider some of the thoughts touched on by this author.

One of the methods of philosophizing is to "fish out" and analyze those elements which are assumed by scientific

(empirical) cognition and which make such cognition possible
at all. The Kantian critical method basically can be reduced
to this. A characteristic phenomenon – philosophers at the
beginning of modern times, when the empirical sciences were
still not yet fully formed, attributed precisely those
features to nature which the sciences later had to assume and
which made them at all possible (thus one can say that these
philosophers in a certain sense were ahead of the method of
Kant). For example, Descartes, directed by the inner logic of
his philosophical system, maintained that final causes did not
operate in nature. As we know, the modern empirical sciences
make methodological assumptions which exclude finality from
the area of their interests. The empirical sciences also
completely abandoned the search for "the essence of things
uncognizable to the senses". This fact was already prepared
and to some extent foreshadowed in the philosophical views of
Locke. As a rule, such views of nature were of joint with the
Greek philosophical heritage interpreted and passed on to
modern times by medieval Scholasticism. Both the rejected
doctrine on the essence of things as well as teleological
causes were something more typical for the Aristotelianism
prevalent in the second half of the Middle Ages. It is here
that the question arises as to the source of the non-Greek
elements so essential for the modern sciences. Foster
perceives this source in the Christian doctrine, and
especially in the teaching on the creation of the world.

The medieval philosopher applied the method of
Aristotle in investigations of nature: he defined the essence
of things, deduced their qualities, searched for final causes.
The Scholastic believed that the world had been created by
God, but at the same time he seemed to forget that the
Aristotelian method for studying the world was based on the
assumption that the world had not been created.

According to Foster, three conceptions of God operated
in Greek theology. The first, God is identified with nature,
or – what amounts to the same thing – nature has divine
features; second, God is characterized only by spiritual
activity, as , for example, the First Mover of Aristotle moves
the world, to be sure, but only as good which attracts things
to itself; third, God is only a Demiurge (as with Plato)
organizing the world. In all of these three versions nature is
given a priori, or as identical with God, or as existing more
or less independently of Him. If nature is (in some sense)
given a priori, then also its features can be deduced a priori

(independently of experience), just as the features of an equilateral trangle can be deduced from its definition.

This apriority of the nature is completely absent in the Christian teaching on the creation of the world. The world owes its existence to the will of the Creator, and no a priori premises can enable us to deduce what sort of world it pleased God to create. The only successful method for cognizing the world is to empirically "see" what it looks like (6). The empiricism of modern science has its source - at least psychologically - in the Christian dogma on the creation of the world.

R. Hooykaas presents similar views in a book entitled "Religion and the Rise of Modern Science" (7). In the opinion of this author the passage from the Greek view of the world as an organism to modern mechanistic formulations took place under the influence of the Bible. The emphasis on the value of manual work by the books of the Bible was supposed to have prepared the foundation for both the future development of the empirical methods themselves as well as for their sequel - organized technical activity.

It often happens that, having made a valid observation, we become so attached to it that it distorts our entire perspective. Having recognized the role of non-Greek elements in the formation of the empirical sciences, we cannot forget that the whole of European culture together with its essential component - modern science - has its roots nowhere else but in ancient Greece. It is more than probable that the questions formulated by the Ionian philosophers of nature in large measure determined the character of contemporary science.

4. The Theology of Newton.

In this anthology there are as many as three studies devoted to Newton. The first - by I. B. Cohen (8) - contains a concise, popularly written account of the Newtonian system of dynamics and theory of gravitation. The second study (9) takes up the problem of the philosophical and theological views of the creator of the new mechanics. Religious problems were the hub of Newton's interests. In the catalogue of his works we find as many as 515 titles devoted to theology and philosophy and only 268 from the fields of mathematics, physics, and astronomy. Newton was aware of the fact that the domain of religion is completely different from everything that science investigates; nevertheless, he was convinced that scientific investigations of the world in a natural way lead to a knowledge of God. In "Optics" we read: "The main business of natural philosophy (10) is to argue from phenomena without feigning hypotheses, and to deduce causes from effects, till we come to the very first cause, which certainly is not mechanical."

Newton's world system is creationistic and mechanistic. At a certain moment of absolute time and in certain place of absolute space God created masses and gave them movement. The creative activity of God is the reason for the rational order which prevails in the world and which makes possible the study of the world by the exact sciences. The Universe could never have risen out of chaos solely through the operation of the laws of mechanics, "though being once formed, it may continue by those laws for many ages" (Optics). In just this sense Boyle often compared the Universe to the famous Strassburg clock. But for Newton God is not only a watchmaker who cares nothing for the fate of the mechanism which He has constructed. Newton understands God's rule over the world not only in the spiritual, religious sense, but also in the sense of "mechanistic" interventions. Here appears the controversial problem of corrections which God from time to time has to make in His work. For example, Newton believes that the visitations of comets in our solar system cause such serious disturbances in the movements of the planets that "blind fate could never make all the planets move in one and the same way in orbits concentric" (Optics). Interventions of the Creator are needed for the further harmonious functioning of the laws of mechanics. This point of Newton's doctrine was criticized by Leibniz, who wrote ironically: "Sir Isaac Newton and his followers have also a very odd opinion concerning the work of God. According to their doctrine, God Almighty wants to wind up his watch from time to time; otherwise it would cease to move. He had not, it seems, sufficient foresight to make it a perpetual motion. Nay, the machine of God's making is so imperfect according to these gentleman that he is obliged to clean it now and then by an extraordinary concourse, and even to mend it as a clockmaker mends his work, who must consequently be so the more unskillful a workman, as he is oftener obliged to mend his work and to set it right." (11).

The problem of "corrections" disappeared from mechanics in the works of Laplace. This scientist believed that he had completely succeeded in showing the "stability" of the world governed solely by the laws of mechanics (12).

The mechanistic picture of the world achieved ever greater triumphs. All that still remained, as Burtt writes, was to accomplish the "mechanization of existence", to introduce the laws of mechanics to the area of the human spirit. And in time this was to happen. "Clock-wise Naturalism" reached its apogee in the period of the French Enlightenment.

5. A New Perspective.

In pre-Newtonian times hypotheses of a scientific character usually grew out of philosophical views. Now the situation was reversed: based on the new science a new philosophy began to emerge. An attempt was made to organize the achievements of mechanics into the most compact, overall picture of the world possible. Simultaneously, the process of the popularization of science went into high gear. Locke observed that none of his contemporaries read Newton, but everyone debated him.

Widely read in those times was Fontenelle's book "The Plurality of Worlds", published in France in 1686, two years later translated into English, and in the course of the next century republished at least twenty times. The author did not treat the technical details of the new science; he was under the influence of the perspectives which the new science opened up, and this is what he expressed. The Earth had ceased to be the center of the Universe and had become its remote province. Man is an insignificant episode in the mechanism of the Cosmos. Since from an astronomical point of view the Earth does not essentially differ from the other planets, life can also exist on them.

A similar argument was used by another writer of this epoch, Thomas Burnett: if medical knowledge acquired through the dissection of one human body can be successuffly applied in the treatment of another individual, then - analogically - knowledge acquired through the study of one planet - the Earth - should be also applied to other planets ("The Sacred Theory of the Earth", 1816). Still another author of the Newtonian period, Charles Blount, maintained that the multiplicity of inhabited worlds was more in keeping with Divine omnipotence and goodness than an empty Universe inhabited only by people on Earth ("The Oracles of Reason", 1693).

The Bible neither confirms nor denies the existence of life on other planets, and only those theologians who would maintain that the entire truth is contained in the Bible could have any trouble with this problem. A traditionally oriented theologian, Robert Jenkin, who, nevertheless, was not an opponent of the new science, attempted to show the concordance between the hypothesis of the multiplicity of worlds and the Christian truth of redemption ("The Reasonableness and Certainty of the Christian Religion", 1700).

But even in theology accents began to shift under the influence of the new achievements of science. The attention of the theologians of this period was more drawn to the truth on the creation of the world by God than to the dogma of redemption. This was in keeping with the spirit of the times. Creation was treated a little like a theological "mechanism" explaining the existence of the world.

An interesting phemomenon in English theology of this period are the famous sermons of Thomas Chalmers of Glasgow. It is said that on Thursday afternoons in 1816 when Chalmers was speaking in Tron Church, all the shops were closed and traffic in the city came to a standstill. Chalmers' "Astronomical Discourses" then represented a very modern theology. Even today some of the thoughts still have a fresh flavor; for example, when Chalmers persuades his listeners that in different fields of cognition one should be guided by different methods of argumentation and that the purpose of Revelation is not to inform people about "distant places of the Universe", but to assure man the means to unite with God (13).

But the new science also permitted atheistic interpretations. Though the apologists of that period all too often emphasized that every mechanism - and hence also the Universe - must have its constructor, for many intellects the idea of the world as a self-constructing machine was something very attractive. In this way the most fundamental truths of Christianity were attacked. The need to take defensive measures arose. It is not by chance that precisely during the seventeenth century Christian apologetics assumed a form which until recently was still taught in schools and universities run by the Church (14).

A certain parallel suggests itself: once again in the course of history man experienced the immensity of the Universe - in the second half of the twentieth century, after the first space flights. I doubt whether man's flight into space has had any significant influence on the philosophy and theology of our times, but for the broad masses this spectacular takeoff was an event comparable to the opening of new horizons by the successes of modern physics and astronomy in the seventeenth and eighteenth centuries. Today books and brochures appear in millions of copies spreading as sensations ideas essentially not different from what was a novelty for Fontenelle, Burnet, Blount, Jenkin, or Chalmers.

6. Concluding Remarks.

The book "Science and Religious Belief" also contains equally interesting articles concerning conflicts between religion and the geological and biological theories of the seventeenth and eighteenth centuries. Since I do not feel competent in these fields, the final parts of the book I leave without comment. In this way the reading of "Science and Religious Belief" has changed into a study of a stage in the history of human thought, fully deserving the name "mechanistic revolution". The mechanism which was born at that time remained dominant until the end of the nineteenth century. Succeeding engineers continued to improve the world machine constructed by Newton. After Laplace's measures it appeared that the machine could function without "God's corrections". To be sure, in the nineteenth century it was understood that perpetuum mobile cannot exist, but people tried to hold on to the belief that the mechanism of the world as a whole is an exception to this rule. Toward the end of the nineteenth century the cosmic machine began to rebel, and at the beginning of the twentieth century the myth of screws, gears, and belts governing the Universe fell apart completely. The new scientific revolution resulted in a departure from mechanism. Mechanism collapsed as few other ideas in philosophy.
Nevertheless, the period of the dominance of mechanism was an important stage in the formation of our conceptions. It was then that the conflict science-faith crystallized, and just this mechanistic phase of the conflict to this day has remained imbedded in the consciousness of many (if not most)

people. Furthermore, current opinions on the subject of the relations between science and religion in the past are shaped rather through a backward projection of one's own experiences or intuitions than through a thorough study of the problem. But such study is necessary, since - first - the examination of past disputes more easily facilitates a neutral objectivism than the experiencing of contemporary disputes, and - second - certain lessons of the past can be easily transposed to today's changed conditions. An error repeated is four times as costly.

Five:

Criteria of Meaning

1. Introduction.

We must return to the problems raised by neopositivism. Though most professional philosophers have cast aside this trend in its most extreme form, it still remains rather tempting for those educated in experimental sciences and technology. The temptations of extreme empiricism are ardently avoided by metaphysicians and theologians, and for the simple reason that their profession is endangered. For example, it is safer to discuss with Duns Scotus or to combat the Montanists than to face trends with which discussion becomes something more than an academic art.

I took down the book of A. J. Ayer "Language, Truth and Logic" (1). How precisely this opuscule, published for the first time more than forty years ago, reflects views that many people of today regard as original! And for this reason the book deserves a more careful reading.

Alfred Ayer lived in Vienna when Schlick's seminar was being held there. Ayer's subsequent scientific career is associated with England, especially with Oxford University. Viennese positivism was complemented by trends which emerged from British analytical philosophy. In sum, this produced a thinker of uncompromising views. The book "Language, Truth and Logic" can be regarded as an abbreviated English version of Viennese neopositivism (2). "Being in every sense a young man's book - Ayer admits in the Introduction - it was written with more passion than most philosophers allow themselves to show, at any rate in their published work." And though today the author is inclined to believe that the problems raised are not as simple as seemed to him before, nevertheless, according to him, the point of view presented remains basically correct.

2. Elimination of Metaphysics.

If one wishes to combat the view of a metaphysician who asserts that he possesses knowledge of reality beyond the world of phenomena, one should not - in Ayer's opinion - ask him on what premises this knowledge is based, but point out the nonsense of his statement. Questions about "arguments" or "proofs" lead to unending discussions; the problem of sense or nonsense can be resolved by only one criterion. According to Ayer, this criterion is verifiability. "We say that a sentence is factually significant to any given person, if, and only if, he knows how to verify the proposition which it purports to express, that is, if he knows what observations would lead him, under certain conditions, to accept the proposition as being true, or reject it as being false." On the other hand, if a so-called assertion is of the kind that both the assumption of its truthfulness as well as the acceptance of its falsity agrees with every observation and if, moreover, the statement is not truly tautological, then it is only a pseudo-statement. The sentence expressing this statement for someone can mean something emotional, but basically it has no literal meaning. Using the language of information theory, such a sentence is noise, not information.

Thus there are two and only two kinds of meaningful sentences: sentences verifiable empirically and sentences verifiable analytically. A sentence is verifiable empirically if to be recognized as true one has to make certain experiments or observations. For example, the sentence "This wall is blue" is empirically verifiable, since to recognize it as true one has to look at the wall. A sentence is verifiable analytically if the analysis of its syntax alone guarantees its truthfulness. For example, "This wall is blue or is not blue". This sentence is true (by virtue of the properties of the alternative "or") apart from what the wall is really like. Such sentences are also called tautologies. Verifiable empirical sentences enter into the system of the empirical sciences, whereas all assertions of logic and mathematics have the character of tautologies. Since sentences expressed by a metaphysician are not verifiable either analytically or empirically, they de facto have no meaning. With the self-assurance typical of early neopositivism Ayer believes that the question of metaphysics has been resolved once and for all - negatively.

3. The Task of Philosophy.

What then should philosophy deal with? Certainly not with the study of the world. Information about the world can only be acquired through the formulation of verifiable empirical sentences, and this is precisely the domain of the empirical sciences. There is no source of knowledge of the world beyond experience. The role of philosophy reduces itself to clarification and analysis of language through which we express knowledge acquired with the help of ordinary experience and - above all - scientific experience. In other words, the task of philosophy is to define terms and thereby introduce clarity to the system of knowledge acquired from somewhere else (not by philosophical methods).

However, a philosophical work differs from an ordinary dictionary which explains the meaning of a given term by giving its synonyms. The philosopher - in Ayer's opinion - does not define by giving synonyms, but by showing how a statement in which a given term meaningfully appears may be replaced by an equivalent statement in which neither the given term nor its synonym already appear. For example, the statement "A square circle cannot exist" is equivalent to the statement "No thing may be simultaneously square and circular".

But from one aspect a philosophical work does resemble a dictionary. Both a philosophical work as well as a dictionary may contain only reporting definitions, not projecting ones. A projective definition is invented (projected) by the author arbitrarily; from then on he must only adhere to the once accepted convention. This is how the mathematician proceeds when for the first time he introduces a new concept to a theory which he has constructed. A definition is reporting when it gives an account of an already existing meaning, one which is in use; here the task of the author reduces itself to culling out (from the context, parallel places, manner of use, etc.) the meaning and using it

65

faithfully in a definition. The philosopher cannot design a definition, for then he would commit the error of the metaphysicians: his "system" would not reflect reality but his own linguistic conventions. The philosopher must construct reporting definitions, i.e. grasp the meaning inhering in everyday and scientific language. Only then will philosophy contribute to a more complete understanding of what we know about the world and life.

From the above considerations one can see why philosophy of language (also called analytical philosophy) is the direct heir of the neopositivistic traditions.

4. A Critique of Value.

The consequences of the nepositivistic constriction of philosophy extend to the field of ethics and religion. The central concept of ethics is the concept of value. Ayer maintains that all statements concerning value either have meaning, but then they are not ethical statements but simply scientific ones (from psychology or sociology), or they are not scientific statements, but then they are meaningless.

In the ethical systems formulated by various philosophers one can distinguish - according to Ayer - four kinds of completely separate statements. First, statements concerning definitions of ethical terms; second, descriptive statements of so-called moral experiences; third, exhortations to moral behavior; fourth, statements expressing value judgments.

It would appear that the core of ethics are value statements. However, these statements cannot be translated into empirical statements, and neither do they have the nature of tautologies. That something is ethically good or bad results neither from any experiment nor from an analysis of the concepts themselves. And thus in accordance with the neopositivistic criterion of meaning, value statements are pseudo-statements, declarations at bottom lacking sense. The presence of an ethical qualifier in a statement adds nothing new to the content of the statement. The utterance "You have done wrong in stealing money" means exactly the same as the statement "You have stolen money", while the attached valuation ("you have done wrong") produces only such effect as, for example, an appropriate intonation of the voice expressing disapproval. An exclamation point or tone of voice render no meaning; at most they are the external expression of someone's emotional state. In this manner what had seemed the core of ethics has been eliminated from ethics understood as a science.

The same concerns various kinds of appeals to ethical behavior. They are not meaningful statements, but only something in the way of means to influence someone to act in such and not another manner.

And what of the remaining categories of ethical statements? Descriptive statements of so-called moral experiences may contain real meaning, but then they belong to psychology or sociology and not to ethics. In real ethics there remain only definitions of ethical terms. Ethics is reduced to a collection of essentially arbitrary definitions. "We find - Ayer writes - that ethical philosophy consists simply in saying that ethical concepts are pseudo-concepts and therefore unanalysable."

While the neopositivists made a critique of ethical philosophy, this does not mean that they approved moral anarchy. Does this mean the resignation? Does this mean that there are no moral directives, that everyone can do what he pleases? - asks another positivist, Reichenbach. And he replies: I do not believe so. On the contrary, to derive from the fact that ethics cannot be objectively proven the conclusion that everyone may do as he pleases shows a lack of understanding of fundamental moral deirectives. (3)

5. A Critique of Religion.

The neopositivistic criterion of meaning results in no lesser devastation in the field of religion and theology. Religious knowledge - in Ayer's opinion - is basically not different from metaphysics, and hence must share its fate, vanishing once and for all from the area in which one can employ expressions containing any meaning whatsoever.

The existence of God, who by definition is Transcendental Existence going beyond all experience, cannot be derived from any empirical data. And does it result from any principles a priori? The only justification by which a certain statement may be true a priori is the tautological nature of that statement. And from a collection of tautologies one cannot deduce something which also would not be a tautology, and thus there is no - for there cannot be - a priori proof for the existence of God.

Since the statement "God exists" is neither a tautology nor an empirical statement, it has no meaning; it is not a statement at all. Ayer notes that this is by no means an argument in favor of atheism, or even agnosticism, since also the statements "God does not exist", "I do not know whether God exists" are equally lacking in meaning. "For if the assertion that there is a god is nonsensical, then the atheist's assertion that there is no god is equally nonsensical, since it is only a significant proposition that can be significantly contradicted." As far as the agnostic is concerned, although he refrains from either asserting or denying God's existence, "he does not deny that the question whether a transcendent god exists is a genuine question. ... And this means that agnosticism also is ruled out."

The same critique strikes at all of the other utterances of a religious type. This has direct consequences for the problem which interests us: science-faith. The antagonism between religion and the sciences is lacking in any logical grounds whatsoever. There is no opposition between science and religion since the religious utterances are not genuine propositions and they "cannot stand in any logical relation to the propositions of science".

Ayer's arguments showing the impossibility of any real conflicts between faith and knowledge are small consolation to the believer. At bottom, they destroy one of the most important motives for accepting religious faith - the genuine meaningfulness of religious convictions.

When someone makes a statement, one can point out his ignorance on two levels, as it were. First, proving that he is wrong, that his statement is false; second, maintaining that the entire problem is meaningless. There is no worse way than this second one to demolish an opponent.

6. The Epilogue to the History of Philosophy.

The attractiveness of neopositivistic philosophy lies also in its condensed simplicity. With the help of only one criterion of meaning one solves immediately, and in most radical fashion, all of the most important problems that have been plaguing mankind for centuries: the problem of ethics, religion, practically all philosophy. Of course, in denying

meaningfulness to these problems the range of possible
investigations is radically narrowed, but this is the price
which may be worth paying for an effective - at least
extemporaneously - assuagement of human anxiety. In this way,
all of the more important philosophical disputes are
automatically resolved.

In the ancient dispute between rationalism and
empiricism the rationalists are wrong when they maintain that
a priori statements can exist which could tell us something
about the real world, but the empiricists are also wrong when
they assert that all true statements are derived from
experience, for there are tautologies which, though they say
nothing about the world, they guarantee their truthfulness in
and of themselves without reference to any experiences
whatsoever.

What is not empty metaphysics in the dispute between
realism and idealism reduces itself to the logical analysis of
existential sentences (i.e. sentences of the type: "X
exists"). Likewise, left over from the dispute between monism
and pluralism are only several lingusitic-logical problems
concerning statements on the relations of parts to the whole
and parts between themselves.

The criterion of meaning acts very selectively. What
has not been rejected by this criterion is clear and
understandable (Descartes would be pleased!). The history of
philsophy has reached its conclusion. Only a collection of
specific problems from the field of the logic of language
still awaits the unflagging effort of a generation of
analysts. And if some philosopher desires to go beyond
language and contribute to the real growth of human knowledge,
then he must become a natural scientist and study the world
with empirical methods. This is the moral contained in the
last sentence of Ayer's book. Is this sentence a tautology or
the result of experience?

7. Caught in Their Own Trap.

In the last, somewhat ironical, remark is a
significant truth. The neopositivistic criterion of sense
itself (meaningful are either tautologies or empirical
statements - tertium non datur) is neither a tautology nor
empirical statement. Hence it should be included within
metaphysics. Thus if one wishes to reject metaphysics with the

aid of the neopositivistic criterion of sense, then one must accept this criterion, and since the criterion itself is metaphysics, one must accept metaphysics. The above reasoning, as an example of a beautiful tautology works both directions; we can make the statement: a necessary and sufficient condition for the rejection of metaphysics is its acceptance. In this way the philosophy represented by Ayer is hoisted with its own petard.

Where is the error which leads to such clearly paradoxical results? One can call on assistance from the theory of language and metalanguage. The criterion of sense, though it applies to language, i.e. establishes the meaningfulness or senselessness of the utterances of a certain language, itself belongs to metalanguage, i.e. to the language of language. One cannot intermingle linguistic levels: the criterion of the sense of linguistic utterances does not refer to metalinguistic statements; the criterion of sense cannot define its own meaningfulness.

Even if these logical entanglements could be unravelled, there are still other snares which the neopositivists have set themselves. Let us recall that, according to Ayer, philosophy should introduce preciseness and order to human knowledge by defining various linguistic terms. But these are to be reporting definitions, not projecting ones; they are to show how a given term is used (in science or in daily life), and not to design new definitions for it. In everyday language there appear the terms, among others, "sense" and "meaning" (for the present we treat them as synonyms). And it is precisely here that neopositivists comitted an inconsistency that later bore its fruit. For the term "sense" ("meaning") they designed a new sense, without considering in what sense the term is used in the presently living language.

For example, let us consider the sentence "There is an ether undetectable to any experience filling all the space". Ayer would say that this is a pseudo-statement, a meaningless utterance, since it is neither a tautology nor a statement which can be confirmed or refuted empirically. For by definition the supposed ether eludes all experience. Did the man in the street or the physicist considering the problem of ether in pre-Einstein electrodynamics evaluate this statement in the same way? Of course, both one and the other would say that the words "sense" and "verifiability" have completely separate meanings. Furthermore, both would note that in order to state whether some statement is empirically verifiable one would first have to understand its meaning. Only when I grasp the meaning of the statement "There is an ether undetectable to any experience filling all of space", when I understand the meaning of the individual words and combine them into a meaningful whole, only then can I make a judgement: this statement cannot be verified empirically. (4)

In common language the terms "sense" and "empirical verifiability" are not synonyms. To be sure, one can so design a definition of sense that both of these terms would coincide, but everything that would later follow from this would already only be the study of our own constructions, not that of existing linguistic reality, which is largely independent of the researcher.

Moreover, if we wanted to apply neopositivistic prescriptions strictly and remove from the empirical sciences everything not directly verifiable through experience, such an operation would leave us only a collection of chaotic facts which only our more or less arbitrary decision would qualify as empirical statements. For every scientist well knows that on the grounds of common experience one cannot unmistakably separate what derives from empiricism and what from an accepted theory.

The aim of science is to construct the most all-embracing theory possible. It is precisely such a theory which enables one to understand empirical data and - what plays the most important role in science - to design new experiments and predict their results. A theory is never either the sum of empirical data or their mere generalization. A theory in a very important way goes beyond empiricism, for it contains elements in various degrees removed from experience, among them elements so far removed that one can justifiably call them purely theoretical. A theory, of course, must have contact with empiricism, but for a long time it has been known that the entire body of a theory is not co-terminous with experience, but only touches it at a relatively few points. Quite true that these are critical points for a theory without which it could not be a scientific theory, but it is also true that without the "theoretical superstructure" these "critical points" would become a useless instrument unable either to explain the world or to predict new experiments.

The dispute between rationalism and empiricism has not ended. The matter still concerns maintaining the proper proportion between reason and empiricism. It would seem that the development of science in the direction of growing levels of abstraction and generality more and more tilts the scale in the direction of rationalism.

Such a state of things seems to undermine the sharp dichotomy between tautologies and empirically verifiable statements. Between propositions appearing from the results of experiments and the assertions of pure logic and mathematics there stretches a broad field of "middle-range truths", which contain elements of more broadly understood experience and aprioriness intermingled with each other "non-linearly". Many people believe that somewhere among these "middle-range truths" there is a place for objective metaphysics and truths of a religious type. I do not intend to defend this thesis; I merely mention it. I hope that I shall have the opportunity to express my own point of view on this question on another occasion.

In this chapter I have only tried to show - I believe successfully - that the problems of sense, questions of ethics, religion, God, the conflict of science-faith, etc. are considerably more complicated than the adherents of logical empiricism (neopositivism) had imagined. These questions cannot be avoided by simply dodging them. In the course of the several decades which separate us from the Vienna Circle and the first edition of Ayer's book the razor of neopositivistic critique has dulled considerably. Moreover, the same critique applied to neopositivistic convictions has shown to what an extent they were undiscriminating in some points.

The history of philosophy still continues to move forward.

Six:

A Superfluous Hypothesis?

1. Is the History of the Universe Cycloidal?

Contact with the Universe very often becomes a temptation for "theological" reflections. It turns out that even looking at the Cosmos through the precise prism of mathematical theories and through the modern telescope does not liberate one from metaphysical inclinations.

William Bonnor is a well-known cosmologist-relativist. His popular book "The Mystery of the Expanding Universe" (1) is read with bated breath. The non-specialist reader will find much absorbing information in Bonnor's book on what the Universe could be like (various possible theoretical world models) and whether it is possible to discover what it is really like (comparison of models with observations). The specialist reader with satisfaction confirms the accuracy of this information and with some pleasure notices that - contrary to the widespread opinions among physicists and astronomers - so much can be translated from the language of mathematical formulas to a literary language understandable to the uninitiated.

An additional attraction of the book is its, in a certain sense, personal character. The researcher maintains his objectivity in face of the problem. He is kept on this track by the tested methods of science: mathematics and experiment. But the researcher is human, has his preferences resulting from one philosophy or another, from such or another "aesthetics of thinking".

Bonnor particularly favors the cycloidal model of the Universe. The equations of the general theory of relativity describe the history of this model as follows. Cosmic evolution begins from a "singular state": the whole mass of the Universe is condensed, mathematically speaking, in one point; infinite density and pressure prevail. Such compressed matter explodes – the world begins to expand, density lessens, galaxies and stars form. But through the whole time gravity is in operation; as a result the rapidity of the expansion gradually diminishes, finally the expansion is completely halted, and the world enters the phase of contraction. The galaxies approach each other, the density of the world grows, taking on ever more difficult to imagine values. During this growing density and pressure all material structures disappear. The world returns from whence it came. In the singular state all matter is again concentrated in one point, infinite density and pressure prevail. In this way the history of the world – and thus the field of research of cosmologists – is contained within two singularities which cannot be transcended.

The function representing how the distance between two arbitrary points of such Universe change in time has the shape of a curve in mathematics called a cycloid (thus the name used by Bonnor for the model). A cycloid is a curve described by a point on the circumference of a circle moving without sliding along a straight line. At the beginning of evolution the distance between any two points of the cycloidal Universe is zero. As the world expands the points under consideration move ever further apart. At the moment when the expansion enters the stage of contraction, the distance between the points reaches its maximum, then begins to diminish until in the final singular state it again is reduced to zero.

Bonnor likes the "cycloidal history" of the world for aestetic reasons, among others. In 1696 the well-known mathematician, Jacob Bernoulli, posed the problem: let us take two points lying on various levels, let us connect them with a smooth wire on which a bead is threaded; what must be the shape of the wire for the bead to move, in the Earth's gravitational field, from one point to the other in the shortest possible time? The answer to this question was found by Isaac Newton, who was then an adviser to the Royal Mint. One day after finishing work he learned of the existence of this problem and solved it between supper and going to bed. It turned out that the curve of the "shortest time", so-called brachistochronic, is a cycloid.

Let us take two points: the initial and final points of the cosmic evolution, and connect them by the "history of the Universe". What "shape" must history have for the world to pass through it under its own gravitation in the shortest time? How beautiful it would be if the answer were: the history of the world should be a cycloid! Beautiful, but is it true?

The world-cycloid has two serious flaws. There are the initial and final singularities. Science wants to know what existed before the initial singularity, but our models do not contain any information on the subject: as a result of the appearance of infinite magnitudes the equations of Einstein cease to be applicable in singular states and cannot be used to extrapolate the model to earlier times. The same difficulty is connected with the final singularity and our curiosity concerning what will happen afterwards.

2. The Theology of Bonnor.

And precisely here are voiced "philosophical" considerations for which Bonnor prefers the model of the world with two singular states, where the phase of expansion is followed by the phase of contraction, to a model with one, only an initial, singular state, where the expansion continues infinitely without returning to singularity. And what will happen – Bonnor asks – if we assume that the contraction of the Universe does not lead to a singular state but is the introduction to a new phase of expansion? The cycles of expansions and contractions will follow one another without end, and the Universe will have an infinite series of oscillations. In other words: while the equations of the general theory of relativity yield a cycloidal model, with a history bounded by two singularities, it could be that – the future development of theory will enable one to join an infinite number of such models, smoothly glue them together, eliminate singularities, and in this manner arrive at an oscillating model, infinite in time. Such a picture of the history of the Universe is possible, since – in Bonnor's opinion – the singular states in the model appeared because, in constructing the model, we assumed too far-reaching simplifications. By accepting assumptions more in accord with reality it would be possible to avoid the inconvenient singular states. There is no doubt - Bonnor concludes - that the initial singularity is completely unreal, and we obtained it, because, first, we oversimplified the problem, and, second, we took too literally the conclusions resulting from this simplification.

There is still another reason - let us somewhat ironically call it theological - why it would be worth eliminating the singular states. For the "unexplained" singular states are a temptation to introduce to cosmology the "hypothesis of God". Indeed, many people identify the beginning of expansion with the creation of the Universe. In a way not precisely known - they assert - at this moment all of the matter of the Universe was formed, which resulted in a cosmic explosion and started expansion. Nor is there any sense to ask about the history of the Universe before this event, since then neither any Universe nor time existed. Bonnor categorically disposes of this kind of interpretation. He says that such a view is false and highly unscientific. For it leads to the conclusion that the beginning of the expansion of the Universe is not a problem requiring solution in a scientific manner, whereas every real problem is a scientific problem in the sense that it is an object of scientific anaylsis and methods. The danger of these ideas consists in that they free us from the obligation of explaining how the heavy atoms were formed, for it suffices to assume that they were simply created in the right proportions. Likewise, there is no need to explain how galaxies come into being from the primaeval matter; they also could already have been present at the moment of creation.

Here Bonnor abandons the problems of cosmological interpretation and and takes up the psychology of theologians. He states that a hidden motive of such reasoning is, of course, the desire to introduce God as a creator. According to him, Christian theology has been uninterruptedly waiting for such an opportunity since the seventeenth century, when science began to dislodge religion from rationally disposed minds. The first stage of such a "dislodgment of religion" by science were the discoveries of Copernicus and Newton, which showed that the laws of mechanics could be understood by the human mind without the help of theology. Then God had to disappear from science of life, expelled by Darwin's theory of evolution. Still remaining to be fought was the battle over the elimination of theology from studies of the human psyche. Embittered theologians of the twentieth century maintain that this field will forever remain immune to scientific studies. However, the experience of past as well as present progress in psychology - in Bonnor's view - allows us to assume that this outlook will turn out to be just as false as all of the previous ones. It is hardly surprising - Bonnor asserts - that in such a difficult time for them theologians enthusiastically greeted the idea that the Universe could have been created some ten billion years ago. A place for God had appeared which had long been sought for.

And here is Bonnor's confession of "scientific faith": Unfortunately, many cosmologists are also inclined to accept this attitude, which is highly deserving of condemnation, because the task of science is to seek a rational explanation for events occuring in the real world, and every scientist who on this occasion refers to God saws off the branch on which he sits. This concerns both the beginning of the expansion of the Universe as well as every other phenomenon. If an explanation cannot be found immediately, then the scientist should refrain from prejudging the phenomenon. A scientist worthy of the name will always be convinced that a rational explanation will someday be found. At the same time, this is the only sign of dogmatism which science can permit itself - otherwise, every problem whose solution would be delayed for several years would open up a broad avenue for biases. The essential truth of this "credo" can be summed up in a well-known anecdote concerning how Laplace, the famous French theoretical physicist, showed Napoleon his book devoted to the mechanics of the heavens, in which he made a detailed analysis of the movements of the planets. Napoleon is said to have remarked: "You have written a thick book about the system of the world without once mentioning the author of the Universe". "Sire - Laplace responded - I did not require such a hypothesis."

3. Critical Remarks.

I believe that Laplace's response is correct if one understands it as a methodological rule. The "hypothesis of God" is superfluous to science, since the natural sciences by definition deal with the study of the material world. Their task consists in explaining observed facts with laws of nature and deriving laws of nature from more complicated constructions called theories. The discovery of a fact or law which does not fit within a present theory calls for the creation of a new scientific theory. This is how the progress of knowledge takes place. If a scientist would attempt to explain some new fact appealing to supernatural causes, not only would he go beyond the competencies of a natural scientist, but he would also commit a cardinal sin against the progress of knowledge. "Proofs" for the existence of God constructed in such a manner would be lamentable.

Thus Laplace's reply in the sense of a methodological rule must be decided completely in his favour. But from the moment when the statement "the hypothesis of God is superfluous to science" is interpreted by someone as "science shows that God does not exist", he transforms a methodological principle into an ontological thesis and engages in metaphysics, which he so much wanted to avoid. It would appear that even Bonnor did not protect himself against this error. One can see this at least in the "propagandist" style which he uses in discussing "theological" problems. Such an accent detracts from the straightforward narration of the other pages.

The English original of Bonnor's book appeared in 1964. Since that time much has taken place in cosmology. In the area of observations A. A. Penzias and R. W. Wilson discovered that outer space is uniformly filled with electromagnetic radiation corresponding to the radiation of a black body with a temperature of c. 3 K (for which these scientists received the Nobel prize in 1978). According to universally accepted interpretation this radiation is a remnant from the very condensed and very hot state of the Universe. One of the greatest theoretical achievements of the cosmology of this period is considered the famous theorems on the existence of singularities proved by S. W. Hawking, R. Penrose, R. P. Geroch and G. F. R. Ellis. (2) These theorems lead to the conclusion that the appearance of singularities in cosmology is not in the last the consequence of simplifying assumptions made during the construction of the model. Bonnor was wrong: singularities cannot be avoided by means of making assumptions more physical.

However, neither the discovery of the blackbody radiation nor the theorems on singularities , strictly speaking, prove that the present history of the world began from a singular state. The discovery of Penzias and Wilson (insofar as its universally accepted interpretation is concerned) only indicates that the Universe at one time found itself in a very dense and very hot state, while the theorems of Hawking, Penrose and others state that singularities cannot be avoided, but under the condition that the present theory of gravitation can be applied to the earliest periods in the evolution of the Universe. The point is that as one moves back to the singularity, when the density of matter grows dramatically, the modern theory of gravity, and perhaps even the whole of present day physics must collapse. The monograph of Hawking and Ellis devoted to the problem of singularities ends with the following statements: "The results we have obtained support the idea that the universe began a finite time ago. However the actual point of creation, the singularity, is outside the scope of presently known laws of physics" (3).

In writing the above words do I feel satisfaction: "and perhaps, after all, a place for God will be found in cosmology?" Not in the least. Recent developments of cosmology only lead me to believe that the problem of singularities is not as simple as Bonnor once believed. Perhaps I would state my reply to Bonnor more simply, but I would prefer (is it from malice?) to make use of the pen of a well-known theologian: "The religious speak of God when human conscience reaches a limit, or when human powers fail (and sometimes from intellectual laziness). In point of fact, God is always understood as a deus ex machina, who is called to make his appearance on the scene either for the ostensible solution of unsolvable problems, or as a power when human powers have failed, and thus always on the occasion of human weakness or on the limits of human cognition. However, quite naturally this can last only as long as people are unable to move this frontier a little further on their own powers and God as a deus ex machina is superfluous. What we say about human frontiers for me is completely questionable. ... It always seems to me that in this way we from fear allot God too small a place. I would wish to speak of God not on the frontier, but in the very center, not in moments of weakness , but in those of strength, not in face of death and guilt, but in face of life and human good. On the frontiers I think it is better to remain silent and leave the unsolvable unsolved." (4)

Seven:

By Chance in the Cosmos

1. A Revelation or an Outrage?

Among the natural sciences biology occupies both a
central as well as a marginal place. Marginal - for the
animate world comprises only a small "fragment" of the
Universe, and the laws of biology do not apply to the regions
lying outside the animate world; central - since science as a
whole ultimately aims at an ever better understanding of the
relation of man to the rest of the world, and in this context
the sciences of life acquire fundamental significance.

Here is the content of the first paragraph of a book
by J. Monod "Chance and Necessity" (1). For several years this
popularized scientific work has not disappeared from
bestseller lists. Translated into several languages it enjoys
an unabating popularity. Jacques Monod, Nobel laureate and
specialist in the field of molecular biology, presents the
achievements and problems of the modern science of the
mechanisms of life and heredity, not hesitating to enrich the
whole with an extensive layer of "commentary" containing the
philosophical considerations of the author. Thanks to a
splendid effort at popularization a broad circle of readers
could almost tangibly come into contact with the successes of
modern biology. All the more suggestive, then, is the layer of
commentary connected with people's outlook on life, presenting
views which are - at least insofar as the so-called philosophy
of science is concerned - quite often encountered in
scientific circles. For many readers these views became a
revelation, for many others - an outrage or a shock.

I do not wish to scandalize or engage in illusions.
Nor do I feel qualified to comment on questions on biology. If
I venture some remarks in this field, they will rather be in
the nature of a reporting of Monod's views, and this mainly
from the point of view of the "physics of life". On the other
hand, I should like to reflect somewhat more deeply on some of
the subjects touched on in "Chance and Necessity", those for
which science is only a point of reference. Monod himself
warns against confusing certain ideas only suggested by
science and the achievements of science itself. The view which
modern biology suggested to him Monod calls ideological
generalizations. These generalization cover a broad field
from loose reflections, through the field of philosophy and
epistemology of science, and all the way up to digressions
concerning religious, and even political beliefs.

Involuntarily I read Monod's book from the point of
view of the problem of science and faith. To be sure, as
regards subject matter this problem is not a central theme of
the book, but it is somehow present on nearly all of its
pages.

2. Vitalisms and Maxwell's Demon.

The distinctness of the phenomena of life from
everything that we know and the fact that we ourselves are its
participants - these are the main reasons for the appearance
of numerous philosophies searching for the so-called essence
of life. In the second chapter of his book Monod presents an
overview of philosophical positions meriting, in his opinion,
the names vitalisms or animisms. Included here are the
opinions of various natural scientists, according to whom the
phenomena of life cannot be completely explained with the help
of the laws of physics (Driesch, Elsasser, Polyani); Bergson's
philosophical doctrine of "elan vital" - life force, not only
distinct from physical forces, but contending with the world
of inanimate matter; the vision of Teilhard de Chardin, in
which, besides ordinary physical energy, appears a
non-physical energy driving the process of evolution; the
materialistic interpretation explaining the appearance of life
and its development through the laws of dialectics.

In Monod's opinion, it suffices to explain the
phenomena of life if one accepts only such an "intelligence"
as Maxwell's demon possesses. Maxwell placed his demon near a
small slot in a wall separating a cylinder into two chambers.
One chamber is empty, the other contains gas. When a rapid

particle (with great kinetic energy) approaches the slot, the demon opens the flap and admitts the particle into the second chamber; when a slow particle (with low kinetic energy) approaches the slot, the demon closes the flap, and the particle remains in the first chamber. Due to the demon's activity after a time energy becomes concentrated in the second chamber, only rapid particles are found there. As a measure of the concentration of energy one can take a certain function in physics called entropy: the higher the concentration of energy, the lower the level of entropy of a given physical system. Thus the operations of the demon result in a lowering of entropy; in the cylinder the level of organization (arrangement) increases: the rapid particles are separated from the slow ones. This remains in open contradiction to the second law of thermodynamics, according to which energy dissipates rather than concentrates, entropy grows rather than diminishes, organization disintegrates rather than forms. For this reason it was also believed that the cognitive activities of Maxwell's demon clashed with the laws of physics. More recent research (Brillouin and Szilard), however, has resolved this apparent paradox. After all, the demon must receive information about the velocities of the approaching particles, and thus must measure these velocities in some way. The energy which must be used in the act of measurement completely cancels out the ostensible gain; the laws of physics are retained; information (order) can grow, but only at the cost of consumed energy; local entropy can diminish, but "for this" somewhere else it grows with excess, so that in the average it is still always increasing. (2)

Life must use the same strategy. Proteins on a microscopic level perform "demonic" functions. But here as well the growth of arrangement (information) does not occur without cost, but at the cost of chemical energy. Life is an anti-entropic process, but on general balance the entropy of the Universe grows. Life processes are reduced to "biochemical cybernetics". The laws of biological structures are the logic of Boolean algebra and not the dialectic of Hegel.

The biochemical cybernetics of life has only taken its first steps, but - in Monod's opinion - "today one can state that the elementary mechanisms of evolution are not only fundamentally understandable, but also identified with precision". If there are still so many things that we do not know, it is because of the unparalleled complexity of the phenomenon of life. (3)

3. The Number That Won at Monte Carlo.

The "ultima ratio" of life - as Monod writes - has been discovered. The elementary mechanisms of evolution have been studied. Evolution is no longer on the "frontier of knowledge". Frontier problems today are the "extremes" of evolution: the appearance of the first living organisms and the appearance of the central nervous system of man, and not the fact of evolution itself.

The questions of the origins of life teem with unusually difficult problems. Among the most difficult certainly is the problem of the coming into existence of the genetic code and the mechanisms of its translation. "In fact here one should not speak of a 'problem', but rather of a genuine enigma." The information coded in the genes would be meaningless if the organism were unable to decode it, to translate it into the language of processes of implementation. Meanwhile, the machine for decoding the code is itself a product of this code; in other words: the information containing the plan of the machine-reader of the code is itself coded and must be read in code. This is a modernized version of the old "omne vivum ex ovo". How did the closing of this square circle come about? What was the probability of the appearance of life before its coming into being? It appears as if the event which determined the appearance of life happened only once. In such a case, the probability that this would happen before it happened was just about zero. Figuratively speaking: the Universe was too small to give more of a chance for life, and the biosphere too confined to give more of a chance for human consciousness. And yet we exist. Our number won at Monte Carlo!

4. Cosmic Loneliness.

In Monod's opinion the touchstone of the scientific method is the postulate of the objectivity of nature. It means the abandonment of any interpretations whatsoever in categories of purpose or design. Before accepting this postulate science (or, rather, pseudo-science) roamed hither and yon along the roadless tracks of "animism", or it imposed on nature human consciousness and forms of action. Animistic views in former times were formulated in all of their mystical naivete: a humanlike intellect was hidden in nearly every creation of nature. Monod believes that animism exists even today, only in more camouflaged form. Modern civilized societies base their morality on a "mixture of Judeo-Christian ethics, scientific progressivism, and pragmatic utilitarianism". This mixture is nothing other than contemporary animism, it is located "beyond objective cognition, beyond truth, it is alien and at bottom hostile to science". Present day societies wish to benefit from science, but they do not wish to accept the most exalted mission of science: "to designate the new and only source of truth, to demand a complete revision of ethics, the radical rejection of the animistic tradition". Nature is entirely objective, there is no thought beyond man. Man must finally awaken from his deceptive dream and discover his loneliness and complete strangeness in the Universe.

Science not only reveals his loneliness to man, but it is to be the handmaiden of his lonely existence. Science is the only source of truth. Metaphysics and religions are animistic illusions. The modern "official" methodology of the sciences asserts that categories of value, which completely elude all possible experimentation, are beyond the competence of science. If this assertion is accepted, then ethics, for which value is, after all, a fundamental concept, will find itself in an area completely uncontrolled by science. Monod does not agree to this breach in the totalism of science. Here is his crowning argument.

In an objective system (the opposite to animism) any mixture of knowledge and value whatsoever is strictly forbidden. "But this prohibition being the 'first commandment' on which objective knowledge is based, itself is not, and cannot be, objective: it is a certain moral rule, a certain norm. True knowledge ignores value, but in order to be able to create objective knowledge a judgment is necessary, or rather an axiom concerning value." The acceptance of such an axiom is a moral choice. "In order to establish a norm of cognition the postulate of objectivity defines a certain value which is objective cognition itself. Recognition of the postulate of objectivity means agreeing to the foundation for a certain ethic - the ethic of cognition." This ethic differs from all "animistic ethics" in that it is not imposed on man from the outside, man himself chooses it like axioms in logic or mathematics.

On the last several pages of "Chance and Necessity" the author discusses the social and political implications of the "ethic of cognition".

5. Science and Values.

For many scientists creative work is not only a source of aesthetic satisfaction, but also a philsophical fascination Similar experiences cannot be felt only by reading popularized scientific literature. I believe that the intellectual adventures of each thinking scientist are something like an abbreviated edition of the history of the philosophy of modern science, in the same sense as the development of an embryo is an abbreviated repetition of the evolution of the species. And hence everyone must pass through a stage akin to positivism. The scientific method, which is used on a daily basis, fills up the entire visible horizon, the style of the habit of thinking in the rigors of this method has a tendency to spread to all areas of reality. Some pass through this stage to other more liberal (not as totalistic) views, others remain in it longer, sometimes for good. (One should remember that all sociological regularities are only statistical regularities.)

Positivism resulted from the fascination with the rapidly increasing achievements of physics in the nineteenth and beginning of the twentieth centuries. Biology is only now entering a similar phase of development, and perhaps for this reason views of the positivist type have such an attraction for the biologist. The area of life still unstudied by science was the domain of philosophical, or sometimes outright poetic, visions and speculations; the appearance of life itself was often explained in religious categories as a result of the special intervention of the Creator. Presently this field has been subjected to the massed invasion of biophysics, biochemistry, molecular biology, genetics, cybernetics and other sciences. The victories, perspectives, and areas still not conquered by the sciences are beautifully described in Monod's book. It is hardly surprising that the very fact of initial conquests fascinated those who had a hand in the victories.

I believe that this is precisely the genesis of the layer of views on the philosophy of life in Monod's work. Here still another regularity came to the surface. When a scientist rediscovers views once already earlier professed by philosophers, he generally does not formulate them as precisely as his predecessors. So what? He is not a professional in this field. But in some points precision is especially important.

For example, let us take this principle advanced by Monod: "science is the only source of truth". Immediately the question raised by Pilate comes to mind: what is truth? and all of the intricacies connected with it that caused the positivists to erase the word from their dictionary.

Or the problem of value. And precisely here Monod's views differ most from positivistic tradition. As we know, Monod assumes that the definitions of objective science itself, at bottom, is a moral requirement. I do not think that this is a precise statement. One must rather distinguish here science from metascience. All statements on the subject of science belong to metascience. Rules or axioms defining what is scientific and what is not scientific are metascientific statements. They have a technical, not a moral character, speaking of "value", but only in a very narrow, utilitarian sense: if one wishes to successfully investigate nature, one should use such, and not other, methods; in particular, do not intermix problems of value with research work. Quite similarly: if one wishes to build a good bridge, one must observe such, and not other, principles of statics.

Even if Monod's requirement of objectivity really did contain a moral substance, the ethic constructed on it would be either very impoverished or very arbitrary. The final pages of "Chance and Necessity" bear witness to this, for nearly every sentence there is highly controversial. Both Comte, the father of nineteenth century positivism, as well as the neo-positivists of the Vienna Circle passed through the phase of wanting to reform society in the name of a "scientific ideology". With indifferent results.

Science is silent on values, though itself is certainly a great value for humanity.

The task of religion is not to supply man "from above" with information about nature. Above all, it is not the task of religion to fill in the gaps in our knowledge (such gaps today are certainly the problems of the beginning of life and consciousness) with speculations concerning the exceptional intervention of the Creator. The task of religion is surely to place man within a specific nexus of values, also creating a suitable climate for scientific inquiries.

Recapitulation

The two revolutions, the mechanistic revolution in the seventeenth and eighteenth centuries and the far-reaching changes which took place in science at the turn of the nineteenth and twentieth centuries, signified new stages in the dispute between "science and faith". During the mechanistic period clashes took place between the particular results of science and certain precisely formulated religious or theological assertions. Neo-positivistic philosophy emerged as a side-effect of the scientific revolution of the turn of the present and past centuries; it questioned religion (and theology) in the aggregate, simply denying the sense of all of its assertions. This is the heaviest blow which can be levelled at religion.

The key issue is the criterion of sense. For the neopositivists the one and only one criterion of the sense of any statement whatsoever (if it is not a tautology) is empirical verifiability. Assertions of the religious type are not empirically verifiable, hence they are meaningless.

But the extreme formulations of the neo-positivists did not withstand the test of time. Their excessive radicalism backfired against them. If its own criteria are applied to the neopositivistic doctrine, it turns out that it is metaphysics (in the pejorative sense of the word) lacking in sense. Neopositivism today , in its extreme form, belongs to trends which among professional philosophers have been superseded, but vulgarized forms of neopositivistic doctrine continue to exist in broad circles of philosophers for their personal use.

Two concrete examples of clashes between science and religion, emerging in the wake of the theory of cosmic evolution and the theory of biological evolution, taught us a certain prudence: the "hypothesis of God" must not be inserted within the gaps of our knowledge. Empirical sciences - by definition - deal with the study of the material world. The discovery of an area which cannot be fitted within present theories enjoins us to improve theories or to create new ones, and not to supplement their deficiences by appealing to supernatural causes.

But this is a purely methodological postulate. The acceptance of the empirical method in the sciences automatically, as it were, obligates us to remain silent on Transcendental Existence, that is Existence which goes beyond empiricism. For empiricism cannot touch that which transcends it.

However, if from the obligation to remain silent about God assumed in the methods of science we were to draw the conclusion that somehow the sciences have proved that He does not exist, we would be disloyal to empirical methods by asserting something which they are unable to verify; we would commit the same error as those who use science to demonstrate that He exists.

From the debate with Monod it is worth remembering still another conclusion. This is an important point, and we shall to return to it in later chapters. Now only a preliminary remark. The sciences cannot make pronouncements on the subject of values, for values are appraised and not measured through experimentation. If the word "value" is used in the sciences, it is only in the technical sense: for the attainment of such goal, as experience indicates, this measure is useful (valuable). And since human life without value would be worthless, precisely this dimension - the dimension of value - leads us to the field of religion.

3

TO KNOW – TO BELIEVE

The problem of "science and faith" was placed in a historical and modern context (part I) and examined through the example of concrete clashes (part II). This led to certain, frgmentary as yet, conclusions. Now it is time for more systematic analysis.

Science increases the fund of human knowledge. Faith is man's answer to the challenge of religion. How does "believe" differ from "know"? What are the criteria for the reasonability of faith? Does faith in general have any grounds for existence in face of the continual expansion of knowledge? The considerations of the present part of the book are an attempt to answer these questions.

The word "faith" is ambiguous: it can mean a set of "truths" in which one believes; it can mean an act of faith with which one believes. But even such a narrowed understanding of faith is weighed down by a plethora of various possible meanings. Let us divide these meanings into two classes: belief (conviction) in the ordinary sense (e.g. as when I believe that my number won a lottery) and faith in the religious sense. Philosophers of language deal with the first class, theologians - with the second.

Religious faith cannot be reduced to faith in the ordinary sense, but linguistic analyses striving toward an understanding of "secular belief" may turn out to be helpful in analyses of religious faith.

The first two chapters of this part (chapters 8 and 9) are a kind of overview of the problems connected with philosophic–linguistic analyses of "secular belief". One of the main objectives of the representatives of linguistic philosophy who deal with these problems is to formulate criteria distinguishing faith from knowledge and other kindred areas of human activity. These chapters have the character of a "second hand" account, based in their entirety on the reading of two books. The last chapter of this part (chapter 10) takes up the of the problems themselves, but from the theological side. Here the problems connected with the issue are enriched by a new dimension – the "unmeasurable dimension" of the Gift of Faith or Grace.

Eight:

Belief in the Secular Sense

> "One may not have confidence in one's own senses,
> but one must trust one's beliefs."
> L. Wittgenstein, "Philosophical Investigations"

1. Introduction.

　　People from the street and ladies from drawing-rooms
(as Schroedinger termed the readers of popularized scientific
literature) would be astonished if they cared to realize how
great a part of our knowledge about the world comes from
faith. After all, nearly everything that we read in books is
not our own experience. Even the most precise experiment (the
more precise, the more so!) is based on knowledge acquired
from predecessors. And for that reason it is not surprising
that the philosophy of science, which since the beginning of
its existence has been striving to impose the tightest
discipline of human knowledge,　sooner or later had to take up
the problem of belief.
　　Belief is a very broad concept: from religious views to
private opinions of varying degrees of justification up to
completely banal thoughts - such as "this plane is flying to
Kennedy" - on which everyday life is based. The philosopher of
science from the positivistic phase in the development of the
discipline treated belief as a synonym for irrationality and
unscientific thinking. All statements connected with any
belief whatsoever must be eliminated from science! The
possibility of realizing this program very quickly turned out
to be yet another positivistic illusion. Since the "element of

93

belief" cannot be avoided either in daily life or in science, one should subject this problem to philosophical control and not allow it to grow wildly. Hence the continual growth of interests in problems connected with belief on the part of methodologists. One can already even speak of a separate chapter in the philosophy of language. A classical problem discussed in this chapter is the issue of belief and knowledge, how their differ and how they are alike, whether knowledge can exist without belief, belief without knowledge, etc. It must be noted that as a rule philsophers of language do not deal with belief in the religious sense, but only with purely "secular belief", i.e. with such convictions as are accepted on the grounds of indirect evidence. Besides, the very problem of defining "belief" - as we shall see - up today has still not seen generally accepted solutions.

The problem of belief and its role in human cognition interested the analytical philosophers, above all. They assert that linguistic analysis is the only instrument able to deal with this set of problems. As their predecessor the analytical philosophers often mention cardinal Newman and his book "An Essay in Aid of a Grammar of Assent".

The volume "Knowledge and Belief", published under the editorship of A. Ph. Griffiths in the well-known series "Oxford Readings in Philosophy", is an anthology of classical positions treating a tangle of these problems (1). The collection is opened by authors who are already classics: J. Cook Wilson, one of the founders of the Oxford analytical school; R. B. Braithwaite, former professor of moral philosophy at Cambridge and to this day one of the greatest English authorities in the field of the formal methodology of science; H. H. Price, H. A. Prichard - both from Oxford; and others representing philosophical centers of England and the United States. The articles are arranged according to a certain leading idea. For example, H. A. Prichard poses a thesis to which N. Malcolm raises objections. A. D. Woozley makes corrections to Malcolm's argument, while A. R. White draws different conclusions from Woozley's arguments than their author. Hence the volume is not only a representative collection, but also reflects the present polemics concerning the problems which interest us.

2. To Know - To Believe.

In answer to the question "what does it mean to believe"?, belief is usually opposed to knowledge (as

something that is more understandable) and the answer is
sought through the comparative method. Braithwiate astonishes
us. According to him, the statement "I know that snow is
falling" contains the following "intentions" of the speaker:
first, "snow is falling" is a true statement; second, I
believe that snow is falling, and the degree of my belief is
high; third, my belief in the fact that snow is falling is
rational and justified. To be sure, when we reflect upon the
content of the word "know", we easily notice that it contains
a conviction, as though adhering to what we know. This is what
Braithwaite calls belief. Very often the terminology adopted
has a bearing on the solution of a problem (especially in the
field of linguistic philosophy). If we accept the terminology
proposed by Braithwaithe, then all knowledge would contain an
element of belief. However, this is not a generally accepted
terminology.

But one can also reverse the problem. Belief in
something – in Price's opinion – assumes the possession of
certain arguments which make the object of belief at least
probable. And thus belief must contain knowledge about
something. For example, my belief in the fact that emperor
Galba was murdered in Rome in 69 A. D. is based on belief (I
did not witness this fact myself) in the veracity of the
historian Tacitus, the latter in turn on belief in ..., etc.
until finally in a chain of beliefs one arrives at the
testimony of our own senses (I read in the book, I listen to
the lecture of the history professor, etc.), and thus to
knowledge (though the knowledge hardly concerns the emperor
Galba, but the fact of reading or listening itself).

Thus the comparison with knowledge will not be an easy
path to understanding of belief. All the more so in that the
word "know" is hardly understood unequivocally. Cook Wilson
would so wish too restrict the concept of knowledge that it
would contain only what we experience directly. Following this
suggestion one could say that I know that the notebook at
which I am looking is blue, but I cannot say that I know that
two masses are attracting each other in conformity with the
model of the Newtonian theory of gravitation. H. H. Price is
so discouraged by the difficulties in defining the meaning of
"know" that he proposes completely eliminating this word from
the philosophical dictionary.

However, we need not be so radical. The most subtle
probes into various shades of meaning perhaps enrich the
dictionaries of synonyms, but they rarely contribute to an
understanding of the thing hidden behind the words. The

functionality of the ordinary language also consists in its elasticity.

H.A. Prichard asserts that "know" and "believe" do not differ in strenght of conviction but qualitatively. Belief is not only "weak knowledge", it is not something "worse" than knowledge. "Know" and "believe" are two completely separate categories.

There are many practical contexts in which one cannot "know", and since one must act (abstention from action is also action), one should be guided by belief as long as it is reasonable. Now the statement of Braithwaite is no longer surprising that "belief... is practically the most important act of thought".

3. To Believe - To Act - To Want.

In the opinion of many authors the concept of belief is more connected with the sphere of action than with the field of knowledge. This is the direction towards which Braithwaite turns his arguments. According to him, "I believe in this proposition" means the same as: "I entertain this proposition and I have a disposition to act as if the proposition were true". If I believe that strawberries cause indigestion, then - if I am even the least consistent - I shall not eat strawberries. Certainly, the tendency to perform certain actions is the criterion of the authenticity of belief, but for Braithwaite also something more - a part of the very meaning of the term "believe". As the predecessor in his views Braithwaite quotes Bain (1868): "The difference between mere conceiving or imagining, with or without strong feeling, and belief, is acting, or being prepared to act, when the occasion arises".

But even here it is a long way to consensus. Price notes that sometimes someone decides to act as though a certain assertion were true, even though he himself does not believe in it. For example, acting in such a manner is the scientist who defends some theory only in order to convince his opponents of its groundlessness

Feelings and will are often connected with the sphere of action. Are they not a case of an essential component of belief? Authors agree that they are not. Braithwaite thinks that feelings are something basically different from belief, though sometimes they can be regarded as a measure of belief: Strong feelings often accompany strong belief. But not always, of course; I can believe strongly that tomorrow will be fair despite the fact that this is emotionally indifferent to me. Price examines the question whether feelings and strong desires could so obscure clarity of vision that under their influence someone would be ready to believe in the absurd. This author highly prizes the human feeling of consistency, since he is inclined to answer in the negative. Certainly, under the influence of strong emotions one may not perceive certain contrary reasons, but if one does perceive them - in Price's opinion - one cannot believe in defiance of these reasons. Belief is more guided by logic than emotions.

We see how difficult it is to isolate the phenomenon of belief from concepts which dovetail with or are its manifestations. I like the simple, almost commonplace formulation of Griffiths: "action waits on belief, and belief waits on evidence". And here - I think - we come to the central problem:

4. Belief - Truth - Freedom.

According to Bernard Mayo, belief is connected with truth in at least two ways. First, what is believed in may be either true or false; second, even if what is belieced in is false, the believer regards it as true. The very fact that something is believed in does not give the object of belief the quality of truth. This leads to obvious conclusions: It is a bad thing to believe in falseness, and a good thing to believe in truth (Griffiths). Truth should be the object of belief, but not falseness (Mayo). F. C. S. Schiller (1924) somewhat pathetically defined belief as a "natural disposition of the mind to welcome truth."

The connection between belief and truth leads to the problem whether belief is a free act or whether it takes place under a certain kind of internal compulsion. Among others who defended the freedom of belief were: Descartes, William James, Newman, Schiller; speaking in favour of "compulsion" are such authors as: Price, Grant, Evans. Joining this discussion, Mayo correctly notes that the more rational a person is, the less freedom he has in accepting something "on faith", the more compellingly rational motivations act on him. Compulsion in this context should be understood in a specific way: it only means that breaking away from it would be irrational behavior. Hence this is compulsion similar to that which appears in moral obligation; one can behave otherwise, but such an action would be immoral. And this is the reason - in the opinion of the same author - why the theory of belief as a matter of fact

97

must be part of the theory of value.

5. Concluding Remarks.

These are only some, selected problems among the many presented in the book "Knowledge and Belief". The tremendous divergence of opinions of the authors represented in the collection eloquently shows that belief - even narrowed to faith "from daily life" (excluding faith in the religious sense) - is an inordinately complex phenomenon. Linguistic analyses are able to reveal only some of its aspects. When linguistic analysis is carried too far, it is hard to safeguard against the barren juggling of word meanings. Language is only an instrument and should be treated as such. On the other hand, the analysis of language, confined within a certain discipline, may introduce a significant degree of precision to areas where, without it, speculations and intuitions would be rife.

Nine:

Faith for a Computer

1. Do Rats Believe?

An experiment: A cage with two openings, one square and one ovate. The rat locked in the cage is always given food through the oval opening. The cages are changed. In the new cage the openings – also square and oval – are located differently. Despite this the rat continues to seek food in the oval opening. And here is the problem: does the rat believe that he will always find food in the oval opening?

The behavior of a rat in cage is a typical problem for a zoopsychologist, but whether certain reflexes of the rat are training or belief is a question, at least in large part, of a linguistic nature. Robert John Ackermann's book "Belief and Knowledge" (1), begins precisely with such discussions. Ackermann is a philosopher who represents the school of linguistic philosophy. The author's concern is to understand precisely the meaning of "believe that ... "; what difference is between "believe that ... " and "know that ... " and what are the criteria for the reasonableness of belief. The work of Ackermann is not an isolated work. The "guide to further reading" at the end of his book clearly shows that the sphere of these problems has attracted the close attention of philosophers of language.

Beliefs are a very complex phenomenon: if one wishes to use the system of formal logic in their analysis, one should – at least in the first stage of research – greatly narrow the field of investigation. Ackermann calls the beliefs of the rat behavioristic beliefs and excludes them from further consideration. Behavioristic belief also appears in the human world; for example, Mr. Harvey Prol who, watching a match on television, automatically reaches toward the refrigerator, believing that, as usual, he will find a can of beer there. Unconscious beliefs - those which psychoanalysis tries to bring to the surface - are not a subject for analysis, either. The author is interested only in conscious beliefs, that means beliefs which can be clearly expressed by someone who possesses them. Among conscious beliefs the analyses made by Ackermann almost exclusively concern so-called factual beliefs; these are beliefs whose truth or falsity can be determined with the help of scientific or ordinary observation. For example, "I believe that the theory of evolution correctly explains all known biological facts","I believe that Tom is the fastest runner in the city". A drastic narrowing of the field of investigation is the price one must pay for precision of analysis and the hope of attaining correct results.

2. Consistency and Completeness of Beliefs.

　　　　Beliefs are indispensable in everyday life. For example, one cannot do without convictions of the kind: "I believe that the teacher is telling the truth","I believe that the box contains what is stated on the label", etc. The point is for beliefs to be rational. The first condition of the rationality of beliefs is their consistency. A collection of statements in which someone believes is consistent if and only if no two statements logically resulting from the set of sentences accepted on faith contradict each other. The criterion of consistency is relatively simple to formulate. The expression "I believe that ... " can be recognized as a certain operator acting on the statement following "that" (e.g. "I believe that the teacher is telling the truth"). Let us denote the believing person by a, the operator "believe that ... " by B (from Belief), and the statement on which operator B acts by p. Thus, Bap we read as: "a believes that p". Following the symbolism commonly used in calculus of propositions, we can enrich our formalism. For example, the notation Ba~Bap we read as: "a believes that a does not believe that p".
　　　　Most generally speaking, Ackermann's technique reduces itself to establishing the rules for omitting the operator B and reducing thereby a "system of beliefs" to a system of ordinary statements. A "system of beliefs" is contradictory if

100

and only if the system of statements after the omission of operator B is non-contradictory. Ackermann's "test" ensures consistency on two levels, as it were: on the level of what is believed in (the non-contradictoriness of the statements remaining by dropping operator B) and on the level of how one believes (the rules concerning operator B).

The next condition of the rationality of beliefs is their completeness. This condition requires that along with the statements in which one believes one also believes in all of the statements which can be logically derived therefrom. The analysis of this condition does not present serious difficulties.

3. Belief and the Calculus of Probability.

The key question: is what I believe true? The attitude to this question ultimately decides the rationality of belief. However, the point is that if I knew the answer to it, belief would yield to knowledge and the entire problem would disappear. Perhaps precisely for the purpose of avoiding this difficulty Ackermann limits it to the examination of factual belief, i.e. such as in principle can be verified, though at the moment of stating his "act of faith" the believer still has not yet verified it; The believer only has certain arguments for and against.

It would appear that the only available way to formalizing this point is through the calculus of probability. The degree of conviction in the correctness of statement p (strength of belief in p) can be defined as the probability of statement p. This probability is judged by the believer himself on the basis of arguments for and against available to him at a given moment. According to the symbolism used in the calculus of probability, falseness is designed by zero, truth by one, and the degree of probability by a fraction between zero and one. If, let us say, I attribute a probability of 2/3 to the statement p, then I must attach a probability of 1/3 to the statement $\sim p$ (it is not true that p). Of course, it is more reasonable to believe in a more probable statement than in a less probable one. Belief in the statement p is reasonable if and only if the probability of statement p is greater than (or equal to) 1/2.

In reality no one calculates his beliefs through probability; this would appear somewhat absurd. But - let us remember - Ackermann is concerned with formalizing the problem, and in such case the more complicated the situation, the more it must be submitted to far-reaching stylization. However, a doubt arises: In this case does not stylization completely distort the problem? In the case of the probabilistic definition of the reasonableness of belief are we not rather dealing with conjecture than with belief?

The "probabilistic model of belief" seems to lead to paradoxes. Let us consider the following situation. There are three numbered slips in a hat. I am supposed to draw out one of them. What is the probability that I shall draw number 1? The probability is 1/3, less than 1/2, so I do not believe that I shall draw slip number 1. But the probability that I shall draw slip number 2 is also 1/3, so neither can I believe that I shall draw slip number 2. The same, of course, concerns slip number 3. And so I cannot believe in the drawing of any slip (for the probability of drawing each of them separately is less than 1/2), despite the fact that I am resolved to draw and certainly shall draw one of them.

This paradox - called the lottery paradox, which was formulated by H. E. Kyburg - inspired a long discussion among specialists (2). Which is hard to believe!

4. Beliefs and Knowledge.

Knowledge is usually contrasted with belief. One can believe in things of which one has no knowledge. E.g. we do not know whether there are other rational creatures in the Universe besides ourselves, but someone can believe that they exist. However, the relation of "beliefs" to "knowledge" is not a mutually exclusive one. Both knowledge as well as belief remain in a certain relation to truth. The problem turns out to be much more complicated than it appears at first glance.

Knowledge claims that it is objective and social; belief, on the contrary, is supposed to be something subjective and private. This distinction is hardly very manifest. Let us imagine an astronaut who made a solo flight to a distant planet and now assures us that rational beings live on that planet. Is this "social" or "private" information? The answer suggests itself that certainly the next space expedition can verify this, and thus we are dealing with information of a social nature. The counter-answer: and if the first astronaut told us about some individual, unique fact from the history of the inhabitants of that planet? Only by accepting the "dogmatic-empirical" model of belief (Ackermann's term) can one easily separate knowledge from belief. But since the representatives of the modern philsophy of language regard this model as outdated and too one-sided, even such a fundamental problem as the selection of criteria for distinguishing belief from knowledge has remained up to now practically without solution.

Both belief (factual) as well as knowledge are open to doubt. If belief is only a certain probability (greater or equal to 1/2 and less than 1), then the contradictory statement is also always probable (though to a lesser degree). Ackermann distinguishes metaphysical doubts and non-metaphysical doubts. Metaphysically, one can doubt everything; the most obvious fact can be doubted by asserting, for example, that what I am experiencing is only a dream. Non-metaphysical doubts are to some degree warranted. Knowledge which can only be subjected to metaphysical doubts is trivial knowledge. Non-trivial knowledge can always be subjected to non-metaphysical doubt. The point is not for one who knows to always doubt that he knows, but for him to be always open to objections and also ready to refute them.

Two strategies are possible here. Either we require that the "knower" be able to refute all possible objections or that he be able to refute all presently known objections. Ackermann calls the first strategy ideal analysis, the second pragmatic analysis. We would be inclined to associate true knowledge with the ideal analysis, but the author prefers to apply pragmatic analysis; it makes more modest demands, and hence again turns out to be more subject to formalization. In passing Ackermann notes that many barren disputes concerning the nature of knowledge were the result of applying ideal analysis where only pragmatic analysis was possible.

It is striking that in everyday intuitions we see a much greater difference between beliefs and knowledge than in the use of formalized analyses of language of knowledge and belief.

5. The Algorithm of Belief.

In conclusion a few words of commentary. Ackermann's analyses excessively narrow the problem of belief. Simplifying measures and a purely formal treatment of the problem create a situation in which the "belief" investigated by Ackermann could be belief of a computer. Based on these considerations one could write a program, introduce it to the memory of the machine and ask it to juggle probabilities, drop or add the operators "believe that ... " and "know that ... " according to set rules, etc. This kind of game could be instructive not

only as a training for a programmer, but also as a
contribution to the development of formalized methods. But
does such a formal game contribute to understanding of the
phenomenon of belief itself?

Ackermann always uses only a finite set of statements
accepted on the basis of belief. This is as excessive
delimination, but one could agree that we shall examine only a
very narrow "fragment" of someone's convictions concerning,
for example, some one subject. More serious objections arise
in the treatment of belief as probability. If "to believe"
means "to take cognizance of something with certain
probability", then how does belief differ from conjecture,
suspicion, circumstantial evidence, etc.? There is a
widespread custom among scientists to call only probable
convictions belief (e.g. "I believe in the correctness of a
unified field theory"), but this is a certain kind of
mannerism. Rather through belief would we be inclined to
understand a conviction to which we attribute the probability
one (i.e. certainty), despite the fact that we do not have
arguments which could completely prove it. If, despite all,
our conviction is reasonable, it is because we accept it for
some "external" reasons, e.g. we have complete confidence in
the person who gave us certain information. And precisely here
the problem arises: not only in what I believe, but whom I
believe? the question of confidence in someone other eludes
all attempts to formalization.

I am definitely not against formal methods, but one
should remember that belief - even if it says nothing about
religious faith - also has its psychological, social, and
existential dimensions. Belief is not merely a question of
proper recording on magnetic tape.

Ten:

The Multidimensional Logic of Faith

1. Introduction.

As we have seen in the two previous chapters, in the contemporary philosophy of language there is a rather strong trend treating the problems connected with belief. The purpose of studies undertaken by representatives of this trend is to understand the meaning of the word "belief", while the means to this goal – in keeping with the tradition of linguistic philosophy – is the analysis of the linguistic contexts in which the word appears. Analytical philosophers are not concerned with belief in the religious sense, but almost exclusively with belief in the common meaning, which is the source of many conjectures and convictions from everyday life.

Let us contrast two statements: "I believe that tonight I shall be lucky to cards", and "I believe there is a God". We intuitively feel that there are more differences separating these statements than similarities which incline us to regard both of them as statements of faith. In the present chapter I wish to ponder on the specific character of religious belief. Let the point of departure be the question: To what extent can analysis of the language of belief derived from contemporary analytical philosophy be applied to the range of problems connected with religious faith?

2. The Method of Artificial Contrast.

The theological "treatise on belief" has an exceptionally rich bibliography. The diversity of formulations, the range of shades of meaning, the multiplicity of accents, and even the dissimilarity of solutions testify to the tremendous effort of theologians to express in words and bring to order what in essence is inexpressible. From the jungle of schools and tendencies I shall select two contrasting formulations and perhaps even overexaggerate their "diametrical oppositeness". I hope that this overdrawn picture will not be a falsification of reality but its laboratory preparation. The use of the method of applying dyes which will permit us to glimpse what otherwise would remain transparently undetectable.

And so, according to a certain formulation still popular several years ago, the fundamental difference between religious belief and knowledge inheres not so much in the content of what one believes, but in the motives for which one believes. The motive for knowledge – as was said, greatly simplifying the problem – is evidence or proof; the motive for belief – the authority of the one in whom one believes, and as far as religious belief is concerned – the authority of the "revealing God". The quotation marks used in this expression are a vestige of standarized textbook and catechism expressions. The credibility of a witness is based on two qualifications: his knowledge and veracity. Not to believe a well-informed witness who does not wish to deceive would be unreasonable. God, all-knowing and the source of good, fulfills the criteria for a credible witness to the highest extent. Thus belief is something reasonable under the condition that the existence of God and the fact that He spoke to man are first established. Traditional apologetics developed an artful network of arguments which were supposed to substantiate these two "premises of belief" (preambula fidei) and developed its own special "grammar of faith", whose aim was to reconstruct the "paths of the intellect" from introductory premises up to the formulation of the judgment: "I have a moral obligation to believe".

To be sure, theologians always emphasized the role of grace on the way to faith. Besides the "measurable dimension", which in principle is common to secular and religious belief, religious belief has an "unmeasurable dimension" unique unto itself alone. But since this is an unmeasurable dimension, it cannot be subjected to rational analysis; at its threshold the realm of mystery begins. In practice this meant limiting the analysis to only the "measurable dimension", and thus in essence to the same thing which is studied today by philosophers from the analytical school. It is not surprising that the latter often rediscover solutions long since known to traditional theologians. An obstacle to recognizing that these are really "unconscious plagiarisms" is the difference of languages used by religious apologists and analytical philosophers. And linguistic differences - as is known - are among the most inflamed differences which exist.

This style of formulating the problems of religious belief can be called theological scientism. Though certainly conventional and "pigeonholeing", this name suggests two things: the likeness of such a theology to the spirit of analytical philosophy (like scientism, the latter has essential connections with positivism) and the tendency in practice to reduce the whole set of problems connected with belief to a certain "logic of faith" or a "grammar of faith".

In looking for an example we shall go to the bookshelf, but first supply ourselves with a dustcloth. There it is! The once widely read and still very charming "Evenings by Leman Lake" by Father Morawski (1).

"On a terrace under the shade of two spreading acacias just before the blue waters of a lake flashing with the golden glitter of the setting sun" for seven evenings a gathering composed of several persons of various nationalities carried on a somewhat too orderly discussion on religious subjects. The Priest, who spoke rarely and usually at the end of the discussion and primarily for the purpose of placing the dot over the "i", was an enlightened theologian for those times. It is even difficult to find some quotation which would clearly reveal the Priest's adherence to a particular trend in apologetics. During the course of the discussion all of the arguments are given in such logical order that toward the end of the last evening nothing remains for Miss Wilson but to ask: "So, finally, what should we do?" And the answer was given. Certainly not by the Priest. It was stated for him in Spanish by Don Pardoval.

*

The twisting paths of philosophy are always reflected in theological investigations, which add their own new, specifically unique complications to the labirynth of these paths. Theology as a branch of knowledge is closer to the humanistic than the exact sciences, and for that reason humanistic philosophical trends weighed more heavily on its modern development than those which grew out of reflections on the empirical sciences. I have in mind the tremendous influence of different varieties of phenomenology and existentialism on contemporary theological investigations (2). Scholastic distinctions and syllogistic speculations have yielded to phenomenological analyses of the facts of inner experience and the employment of situations of concrete, human existence.

The "measurable dimension" of belief without its "unmeasurable dimension" is a falsification of the essence of religious belief and its existential character. Thus one should relinquish the pseudo-precise analysis of fragments of what is an indivisible whole. Belief is not a formalized system of premises and conclusions but a personal - very personal - contact between man and God. Belief is not only a matter of intellect, but concerns the whole person. Belief penetrates the whole of human existence.

A tremendous field of possibilities opens up here based on making use of analogies with the most intimate relations between people: above all, the love between He - She (on the model of the biblical "Song of Songs"), the terms favored by theologians: encounter, dialogue, answer to values, etc.

We make use of an example. I am holding a book (3) whose ambition - among others - is to make use to the achievements of the philosophy of science to construct a methodology of theology. Here are the author's considerations on belief:

First, there is knowledge born from love. Pascal spoke of this when he emphasized that the heart has reasons which the mind does not know. By mind one should understand a set of functions on the first three levels of cognitive activity, on the levels of experience, understanding, and judging. By reasons of the heart one should understand intentional reactions to values. Two aspects of these reactions have to be recalled: the absolute aspect, which is a recognition of values, and the relative aspect, which is a selection of one value over another. Finally, by heart one should understand a subject finding itself on the fourth, existential level of intentional consciousness and being in a dynamic state of existence in love. Hence Pascal's remark that apart from knowledge of facts at which we arrive through experience, reasoning, and verification there exists another kind of values and the judgements of the valuating person who loves.

While true that this is a fragment torn from a whole and only in this whole would take on its true meaning, what is more, it does not even present a complete description of the phenomenon of faith, but only a certan one of its aspects (the answer to values), nevertheless I fear that the "ordinary reader", i.e. the reader accustomed to associate common meanings with expressions would be inclined to suspect this text of an excess of sentimentalism (knowledge born from love) and a geological obsession for isolating levels (but is this not a sign of theological scientism?). I hardly wish to belittle the value of Lonergan's work; I only wish to call attention to something rather typical of the new theology: an excessive readiness to formulate and divide into factors what in essence is an inexpressible whole may easily lead to an overuse of high-sounding words and, in effect, to somewhat strange associations. Great words very qickly become devalued. This kind of tendencies threaten less experienced theologians and popularizers of theology with the specter of irrationalism. One must take care lest this specter become a reaction to the long period of dominance of theological scientism.

3. A Priori.

How can a proportion be maintained between theological scientism and theological irrationalism? The quintessence of the rationality of man is the science which he has created. Learned "demonstrations" of belief more or less on the model of demonstrations of scientific truths would be a misunderstanding: belief is a "different quality" in comparison with scientific knowledge. On the other hand, however, after the achievements of modern science is there any place at all for this "different quality"? If not, then do we have any right to continue to regard belief as something rational?

The further considerations of this section are inspired by the beautiful sketch of Karl Rahner "Science as 'Confession'" (4). I shall draw thoughts (and quotations) from this sketch, but arrange them into a somewhat different whole, for which, of course, I alone bear responsibility.

Science has a dual a priori: historical and metaphysical. An historical a priori certainly underpins all questions asked of nature, if not all the contents of scientific statements. Science cannot simultaneously move off in all possible research directions. The answers received to the questions posed are not able to inform us about what we have relinquished. The directions of questions is conditioned by the often fortuitous course of history.

"We discover only what can be found in the direction selected by the scientific scouting party. The general direction of the inquiring glance, a direction deflecting beyond an already known circle is not conditioned by the subject itself (after all, certainly not yet apprehended), and thus not by the thing of which science speaks. It is determined by a choice preceding a specific science, a choice which embraces it from the outside and bears it, one can say, 'non-scientifically' and for that reason cannot be summoned before scientific courts. ... Neither individuals nor entire historical epochs can move off in all directions at the same time to discover everything in this manner. Hence each acquisition is simultaneously some resignation, each blessing, is some curse." (5)

Even a protest against one tradition or another is already determined by what is protested against, thus is determined by the past.

But science also has its metaphysical a prioris. Many philosophers believe that all sciences tacitly assume the existence of the objects which they investigate (6). Precisely such an assertion is used to justify the indispensability of various ontologies. The truth is that scientists have a natural inclination to accept such an assumption and quite often - tacitly or openly - really do so, but this is an assumption of scientists and not an assumption of science. Science is completely satisfied with a conditional procedure: "if object X exists, it has the following properties ...". Personally I do not doubt in the existence of the real world, but I do believe that one cannot find sufficient justification in the contemporary empirical method for the replacement of the above conditional proposition with a statement asserting existence. It is another matter that sciences - not toying with metaphysical distinctions - as a rule in their statements omit the antecedent (if X exists), being satisfied with stating the consequent clause (X has the following properties ...).

However, the contemporary empirical method is based on certain real assumptions; it assumes them tacitly, but itself does not supply the means to investigate them. And thus the empirical sciences assume that nature (significantly: if it exists) can be described through the language of mathematics. In other words, there exists a specific correspondence between "material entities" and a certain class of "mathematical entities". Phrased still another way, nature is subject to mathematical laws; or more briefly: nature is mathematical. The assumption of the mathematicalness of nature is a highly metaphysical assumption; it attributes a specific structure to nature.

Speaking figuratively: if science is completely uninterested in the question whether the world exists or not (the dispute between realism and idealism), then the problem whether the world has the structure atributed to it by the assumption of the mathematicalness of nature is a question of be or not to be for all of the empirical sciences.

The assumption of the mathematicalness of nature is sometimes stated in the form of the "law of limitations of possibilities" (7). A world lacking any limitations, a world in which absolutely everything would be possible, would be complete chaos, an anarchy that could not be described through any mathematical relationship whatsoever.

There are tacit assumptions made by empirical sciences derivative in relation to the asumption of the mathematicalness of nature. For example, it is insufficient to assume that the world is described through mathematical functions; the sciences can only exist if the world is described with fair approximation with the help of sufficiently simple mathematical functions. These functions have to be simple enough for us to be able to formulate them and subject them to analysis. This assumption - once called the assumption of the uniformity of nature - is at bottom a statement about something in nature itself as well as about our possibility of cognizing it: the limited human possibilities of cognition and the complexity of nature are such that man is able to cognize nature.

We shall not continue to develop this subject. Important is the fact that science a priori makes certain metaphysical assumptions, which it does not submit to discussion and which, to be sure, determine not the existence of the world, but the existence of the sciences investigating the world.

Thus science has its own historical and metapsyhical a prioris. Religious truth should not be sought among the final conclusions at which science arrives; the conviction of religious truth "has its place in the living reality of man, precisely where the a priori assumptions of science inhere, insurmountable for it and not its subject" (8). The scientific picture of the world is chronologically and logically later than religious belief.

Every person begins his existence in a world which already exists. Every fact is given to man in a context of convictions and opinions known beforehand. The world in which we live is passed on to us by our predecessors; the history of philosophy and science are inscribed on the genes of our views. This is our historical a priori. All attempts to construct our own, empirical picture of the world assume a series of metaphysical assumptions, above all that we can cognize the world. And this is our metaphysical a priori. Then to construct this picture of the world we harness science, and when the period of fascination with its causal results passes, we are surprised to discover that what is most essential for us is not found at the top of the pyramid of scientific achievements but at its base. Rahner expresses this as follows: "... knowledge about God already from the very beginning differs qualitatively from knowledge picturing the world. God is not a part of the world, but its a priori assumption. He is not an objective part of knowledge besides its other objects but an infinity which every aspiration for knowledge assumes beforehand and within which it runs along its finite paths. God is not some final hypothesis which would complete a finished picture of the world, but is the only thesis implied in all hypotheses without exception that are constructing this picture. For always and everywhere in each case the construction of the picture of the world for its singular structures assumes that meaning exists in the plurality of all things, connections and correlations occur, and also in this manner the existence of original and meaningful unity before plurality is confirmed. Moreover, the very recognition that the picture of the world is always limited, open, subject to questioning - the principle by which science lives - is possible only thanks the a priori confirmation, implicite, of some existence confronted asymptotically, infinite, which we call God." (9)

Rahner's view are near to me, though perhaps God did not spring so suddenly from the a priori assumptions of science as their "asymptotic confirmation". I would express my view more sparingly: I believe that a certain interpretation of the a priori assumptions leads to theism, but - also contrariwise - and even more transparently - from belief in the existence of the Absolute certain conclusions follow which for science are metaphysical a priori.

The religious belief is a "different quality" in relation to the propositions of science, but it is also a "rational quality"; its rationality grows out of the same a priori as the rationality of scientific assertions.

4. Zeroth Approximation.

Let us return to the question posed in the introduction: to what extent can analysis of the language of belief derived from the trend of analytical philosophy be applied to the range of problems connected with religious belief?

In the phenomenon of religious faith we distinguished the "measurable dimension" and the "unmeasurable dimension", but the statement that linguistic analyses work well in the "measurable dimension", while being completely unsuccessful in the "unmeasurable dimension", would be an oversimplification. The point is that both dimensions are inseparably united, non-linearly blended. Figuratively speaking, we can distinguish the measurable and unmeasurable component only on the level of a zero approximation to the problem and then in the measurable stratum make use of linguistic analyses. But if we move to successive approximations, the separation of the problem into "components" becomes an artificial and distorting operation.

We have noted a great similarity between the style of considerations of so-called theological scientism of the phenomenon of religious faith and the linguistic studies of "belief" of the analytical school. If we leave aside the "unmeasurable dimension" of religious belief - as theological scientism did in practice - then religious belief becomes something more akin to "convictions" or "belief" in the common sense. To agree to such a simplification may be justified - we stress once again - only when it is accompanied by an awareness that it is a zero (not even first) approximation in the investigation of the problem interesting us.

Even in using only the zero approximation we can see the unusual complexity of the phenomenon of belief. It will suffice to recall the difficulties of the analytical philosophers in defining the term "belief". Belief (from everyday, not necessary religious, life) is not a simple opposition to knowledge in the sense of saying: "what cannot be known can only be believed in"; belief is intimately connected with the realm of values, action and will, and even feelings; According to Ackermann, belief differs from knowledge in that it does not give certainty, being satisfied only with judicious probability.

As soon as we carry the analysis over to the area of religious faith, the extent of the problem increases still

113

further. For example, I think that one can speak of some "uncertainty of belief", but one cannot reduce this uncertainty to the juggling of probabilities. Even if, formally speaking, belief could be understood as probability, then, even so, what is lacking to one (to certainty) in belief is complemented with trust. Trust is not a logical category and may be so strong and so connected with personal values that it goes far "beyond one". Furthermore, trust need hardly be something irrational. On the contrary, we know of situations from our own life in which denying trust to someone would be unpardonable lack of good sense. Expressing the "uncertainty of belief" - if it simply does not mean still immature belief - merely stresses the fact that I am placing the "burden of certainty" on someone whom I trust.

Speaking of trust and involvment in Someone Else, we imperceptibly pass from a zero to successive, higher approximations. We also notice that even more aspects of the problem elude analysis. In theological language the Gift of Meeting is called Grace. Here one can either appeal to personal experience or write many words which will be still further evidence of the ambiguity of human language. Silence is the a priori of each pronouncement.

Recapitulation

Let us first assemble the conclusions concerning the relation of knowledge to belief in the common sense ("secular belief"). In detail, often over-subtly philsophical linguistic analyses show that (a) it is not easy to suggest definition, even moderately precise, of the term "belief"; (b) the boundary between belief and knowledge is fluid, they are blurred: in each bit of knowledge we can detect elements of belief (Braithwiate), and every belief assumes a certain knowledge (Price); (c) belief is closely connected with action, or, at least, with "the readiness to act should a suitable situation arise" (Bain); (d) belief cannot be reduced to probable knowledge (polemic with Ackermann); (e) In comparison with knowledge belief is "another quality", but it can also be rational (reasonable) if it is based on rational motives; (f) the rational motives of belief are "external" in relation to belief itself, appealing to trust in the "witness of belief" (to his knowledge and veracity).

To be sure, religious belief contains elements of belief in the common sense, but it is also something much more. How much more? To what extent in analyses of religious belief can one make use of analyses of "secular belief"? - is a subject of disputes among various theological trends.

The rational motives of religious belief cannot be sought among the conclusions of any science whatsoever, but rather among the "philosophical a priori" of every science.

"God is not an objective part of knowledge besides its other objects but an infinity which every aspiration for knowledge always assumes beforehand and within which it runs along its finite paths" (Rahner).

But religious belief is not only a matter of the intellect. Belief is a personal – and very personal – dialogue between man and God. Belief infuses not only reason and the sphere of action but the whole of man and human existence. Belief is existential in character and is Grace, or the Gift of Meeting.

4

LANGUAGE AND SYMBOLS

Both the content of belief as well as the conclusions (and also methods) of science are expressed in some language. The conflict between science and belief appears primarily on the level of languages. In the previous part I referred to analyses made by lingustic philsophers, but these analyses concerned the narrow problem: what is the meaning of the expression "to believe"? Now, in part four I am concerned with the character of religious language in general. Since studies of language in the sciences are much more advanced than the study of religious (or theological) language, the method of my analyses will be to contrast religious language with the language of science. To contrast, since - as we shall see - the character of religious statements differs radically from the character of scientific statements (especially of the formal and empirical sciences). The key to understanding this difference is to call attention to the specific symbolism of the language of belief.

The first chapter of this part (chapter 11) points out the dependence of the content of the statements on the limitation of language. This dependence appears both in the sphere of man's daily activities and in ordinary language as well as in man's scientific activity and in the language of science. How much more strongly must this appear in the field of religion and the language of belief!

The next chapter (chapter 12) discusses the concept of symbol in the modern philosophy of language and applies it to an analysis of ordinary, scientific, and religious language.

The last chapter of this part (chapter 13) represents a certain concrete attempt (proposed by Ferdinand Chapey) to resolve (or, rather, to sever) the dispute between religion and science based on the unique symbolism of the language of religion. This is a critical presentation, since - in the opinion of the author of these words - though Chapey's proposition introduces many essential elements to the question under consideration, it is not able to eliminate the problem.

Eleven:

In the Bondage of Language

From a children's conversation (real):
Johnny: God has it good. He never has to go out of
the house.
Billy: You don't say! And shopping?
Johnny: He doesn't have to. Why, He can create
everything he needs.
Billy: In any case, from time to time He has
to get some air.
Johnny: (silent, overcome).

1. A Lesson from the History of Physics.

We have a latent tendency to generalize. How often on
the basis of two or three cases known to us "by sight" do we
pronounce general opinions? How many times, guided by the
so-called "first galnce", do we judge a person, and how many
times are we radically wrong? We are inclined to regard our
own observations and intellectual constructions as the common
measure for all of reality.
Philosophy indulged in similar tendencies and still
continues to do so. Hasty generalizations were, and still are,
its too often occuring error. It was relatively simple for
successors to unmask the error of Thales of Miletus, who,
having observed that water is indispensable for the
development of living organisms, immediately recognized it as
the first principle (arche) of all nature. But science had to

develop for a few centuries before the incorrectness of the mechanistic thesis that the mechanics discovered by Newton is able to explain all of the phenomena taking place in the world, became evident. Up to today many thinkers are firmly convinced that evolution is the fundamental law of all reality, though the theory of evolution is sufficiently well-grounded and works well only in the field of biology.

Let us examine somewhat more closely the case of the Newtonian mechanics. Up to and including the nineteenth century the mechanistic thesis was regarded as nearly a dogma (or more than a dogma) of science. He who have dared to profess non-mechanistic views would have exposed himself to ridicule and to the opinion of a scientific heretic. The mechanistic thesis was clearly formulated by Helmholtz: "Ultimately, we come to the conclusion that the task of the science of physics consists in reducing the phenomena of nature to unchangeable forces of attraction and repulsion whose strength depends completely on distance. The solvability of this problem is the condition for the complete understandability of nature." And thus to understand nature is - according to Helmholtz - to fully describe it in terms of classical mechanics. In such an interpretation classical mechanics became a kind of ontology.

Albert Einstein and Leopolod Infeld quote the above statement by Helmholtz in the book "The Evolution of Physics" (1), but immediately thereafter they remark that to a physicist of the twentieth century such a view seems unwise and naive. They would be dismayed by the thought that the great adventure of scientific inquiries could so quickly give way to a dull, once and for all established picture of the world.

This sudden - for it took place in hardly several decades - change of views was the result of the lesson which the history of physics gave physicists.

Attempts at mechanistic interpretation of electrodynamics and the theory of the black body radiation made in the second half of the nineteenth century began to reveal gaps and inconsistencies in the mechanistic program. These gaps and inconsistencies were so great that a deep crisis ensued. But contrary to the pessimistic opinions of many physicists and philosophers of that time, the impasse turned out to be a typical crisis of growth. Difficulties in the field of electrodynamics led to the formulation of the special theory of relativity, difficulties in the interpretation of the black body radiation gave the start to quantum mechanics.

The special theory of relativity revolutionized the mechanistic ideas of time and space. Quantum mechanics overturned the classical dogma of the continuity of energy and once and for all eliminated the possibility of thinking of atoms and subatomic particles as small balls of matter subject to the laws of Newtonian physics.

Was Newtonian physics overturned? Strictly speaking - no. Earlier it had been believed - which was precisely the fundamental assertion of mechanism - that Newtonian mechanics is generally valid and that its range of applicability extends to all physical reality; the scientific revolution at the beginning of the twentieth century did not negate Newton's achievements, but only gave them a strictly limited area of applicability. It turned out that the laws of classical mechanics can be applied with good results only in the so-called macroworld, that is - broadly speaking - in the world of our everyday experience. In the microworld of atoms and elementary particles classical physics fails, there the laws of quantum mechanics are valid.

When we deal with objects moving at moderate speeds in comparison with the speed of light, the application of Newtonian laws gives good results; when we investigate objects moving with speeds close to that of light, Newtonian laws do not agree with the results of experiments; in order to attain correct results the Einsteinian theory of relativity must be applied.

Scientific theories, as it were, divided the reality under investigation among themselves. Here an interesting regularity occurs. Theories in a continuous manner pass from one to the other. When in the investigation of the microworld we examine ever larger areas, take into consideration ever greater collections of atoms, we ultimately reach such dimensions in which the results obtained with the help of quantum mechanics are nearly identical with the results obtained through classical mechanics. Similarly, as the speed of the bodies investigated diminishes the laws of the special theory of relativity differ less and less from the laws of Newton.

In the world of our everyday experience the differences between the predictions of Newtonian physics and quantum and relativistic physics are so minute as to be practically imperceptible to experience; with full confidence we can apply the simplest of all - Newtonian physics. Since for long centuries humanity dealt solely with the world of everyday experience, other possibilities were not considered; common experience was raised to an absolute.

The moral of this lesson from the history of science is quite clear: let us beware of over hasty generalizations; let us remember that our intellectual constructions most often have a limited range of applicability. What appears to us as a gen ral regularity most often is "not valid" beyond our intellectual horizon.

2. The Continuation of the Moral.

The moral from the history of physics is worth developing still further. Classical mechanics came into being from the quantitative interpretation of the experiences of everyday life. The experiments on which Newton based himself in his investigations did not go much farther beyond the apple falling from the tree. The experiences of everyday life are described in everyday, common language; for common language grew out of the need to exchange information on the subject of everyday experiences. It is hardly surprising, then, that the language of Newtonian mechanics was a stylization of common language. The terms: force, mass, speed, energy, acceleration, often appear in common speech. Classical mechanics drew from them, only giving them a strictly defined meaning, but nearly always remaining in a certain agreement with their common meaning.

This close kinship between the language of classical mechanics and common language was still another reason for the belief in the "naturalness" and "absolute validity" of Newtonian mechanics; a belief, which - as we have seen - turned out to be false.

Common speach is our "natural" language, we have no other, and for that reason in the creation of any "artificial" languages, whether in physics or in philosophy, it always remains our base, our point of departure and reference.

Here is a new source of frequent paradoxes and misunderstandings.

The apparatus of quantum mechanics is completely different from the relatively simple mathematical instruments used in classical physics. So different - that nearly insurmountable difficulties arise when we desire to speak about quantum mechanics in ordinary language. But we are compelled to speak about quantum mechanics in ordinary language, if only for the reason that the theoretical predictions of quantum mechanics have to be compared with the results of experiments, and the instruments we make use of in the experiments are macroscopic objects.

122

Therefore, we speak in everyday language about a world which is governed by the laws of quantum mechanics. Involuntarily, we look for some correspondence between the "quantum features" and the features attributed to bodies by classical physics, whose language was formed on the basis of ordinary language. And precisely for that reason we fall into paradoxes and ostensible contradictions. Here is the source of the unending philosophical disputes provoked by the development of modern physics.

For example, it turns out that in quantum mechanics concepts so fundamental for the ontology of everyday language as the concept of the individuality of an elementary particle or its localization lose their common meaning. What are "objects" which do not have their individuality, are not located in any given point of space, etc.? They are something for which we have no term in common language. The features of this "something" are correctly, and without the least contradiction, described in mathematical formulas, which are the "body" of quantum mechanics, but when we try to speak about the qualities of this "something" in common language, we immediately become enmeshed in paradoxes.

"How should one speak about the newly arisen situation?" - asks one of the founders of quantum mechanics, Werner von Heisenberg, and answers: "The real problem, hidden behind a series of such problems which are the subject of the dispute, was that there was no language through which the new situation could have been described without falling into contradictions. Ordinary language was based on old concepts ... and, at the same time, it was the only instrument for transmitting information about the manner of performing and results of our experiments. And present experiments have shown that it is not always possible to use old concepts." (2)

To put it still another way: the language of mathematics is more elastic,it was easily able to assimilate the new logic of quantum theory; common language is rigidly connected with the simple "yes-no" of Aristotelian logic. To avoid this difficulty efforts were made to construct artificial languages based on more elaborate logics, capable of describing the world governed by quantum mechanics. However, in effect new logical systems were attained equally far removed from common language as the ordinary mathematical formalism of quantum theory.

It is not our aim to trace the otherwise fascinating history of quantum mechanics and the philosophical disputes which it engendered. We only wish to understand the general cognitive significance of this important truth: our cognition is zonal, does not embrace all of reality at once, but only a certain limited area of it; the cognitive means at our disposal are successful in this and not in another field; only tediously, step by step, developing new cognitive means do we conquer the next field. The mechanical transference of methods that work in one area to another area threatens to produce conflicts. Above all, this concerns scientific theories, but it also holds true in ordinary cognition and corresponding everyday language, which also has its zone of validity.

3. Language Games.

A feature of everyday language is its great elasticity. We reach agreement in it in thousands of life situations, we pray in it and revile each other in it, we write trade agreements and poetry in this language. Everyday language is alive. Every dictionary or lexicon is already outdated at the moment of its writing. Moreover, only single words can be placed in alphabetical order and they are language to the same extent as bricks are architecture. Language is also larger meaningful wholes: sentences, a succession of sentences, their sequence, the logic enclosed in the construction of this sequence, the cadence of the meanings following each other. But - paradoxically - language is also infused with a certain extralingustic reality: gestures, suspension of voice, intonation can radically alter the meaning imparted by the words.

Precisely this led linguistic philosophers to distinguish (each distinction is a simplification, but the art of thinking consists in the ability to simplify) two levels of language: the superficial level and the deep level (one also speaks of the superficial and deep structure of language). The superficial level is, broadly speaking, what is found in the grammars and dictionaries of a given language; the deep level is the external world of the speaker which more or less modifies, and often openly determines , the meaning of utterance.

In this sense Ludwig Wittgenstein speaks of "language games". A deeper familiarity with language is acquired by manipulating it, just as facility in a game is gained by playing it. "The term 'language game' - Wittgenstein writes in "Philosophical Investigations" - is used here to emphasize that speaking is a part of a certain activity, a certain manner of life" (3).

Here is an example - also taken from "Philosophical Investigations" - illustrating how a "certain activity" or a "certain manner of life" gives "deeper meaning" to such simple, it would appear, expressions as "color" and "shape": Let us imagine that somebody shows us a vase and says: "Look at that azure, the shape is not important", or: "Look at that shape, the color is not imortant". In conforming to these instructions each time one does something else. Sometimes one concentrates on color by shading the shape with one's hand or by trying to remember where one has already seen this color. Sometimes one concentrates on shape by drawing it or by closing one's eyes so that the color would not be visible. "These and similar things take place - concludes Wittgenstain - while 'directing attention to this and that'" (4).

4. Game Confilcts.

In everyday life common language does its work very well. Its deep structure becomes transparent to co-speakers, since their "manners of life" are the same, they are guided by the same rules of the "language game". Though even here not infrequently a "game conflict" occurs. As an example let us take typical areas of family conflicts, the so-called conflict of generations: various "styles of life" of the older and younger generations create a situation where the same expressions (e.g. "life opportunity", "proper placement in life", "opinion of others", etc.) for their representatives take on different meanings. People express this with true intuition: "we cannot understand each other".
Perhaps the majority of family conflicts could be explained by the fact that different experiences and different life activity of the parties in conflict result in divergent interpretations of the rules of language games. And to the contrary: true friends are in accord, for the superficial and deep structures of their language are in mutual correspondence. Friendship is born from togetherness.
Formal languages (logic and mathematics, if these two disciplines are at all different from each other) are lacking the deep structure, everything here is reduced to rules of syntax and the proper dictionary. And for this reason either someone understands these languages in the same way as everybody else or he does not understands them at all.
In this respect philosophy finds itself on the opposite pole. In the languages of various philosophical systems words and statements appear derived primarily from

common language, but torn out of the context of concrete human experiences and activities connected with speaking. Under the external layer of the superficial structure is hidden a very extended deep structure, except that it is not conditioned by everyday activities more or less common to all people from a given cultural milieu, but by philosophical education, the body of digested readings, manners of thinking of a follower of a philsophical trend, the degree of involving and experiencing of certain philosophical contents; in a word - everything which I would be inclined to call philosophical ballast.

Hence the impossibility of reaching agreement by philosophers belonging to various camps. Hence the notorious charge of ignorance levelled against the opponent in philosophical discussions. Meanwhile, this is not ignorance, but the impossibility of entering into the language game of the discussant.

The proverbial antagonisms between philosophers and representatives of the exact sciences or between the latter and those working in the humanities belong to the same category of impossibility.

5. Impossibility in Theology.

It is now time to pass on to theological applications. In light of the above considerations they are almost obvious. Above all, theology shares the fate of philosophy in its dependence on language games.

Theological language is based on common language, but in contrast to the latter is lacking the interpretation of its deep structure in the everyday activities of man. One can summon here for assistance the sphere of religious experiences of man as a certain guidepost in understanding the deep layer of some pronouncements of the religious type (in practice certain theological currents do just this, though they do not refer directly to the theory of two layers of language), but considering the richness, diversity and often impossibility of expressing this type of experience, this would not be a very sure guidepost.

This difficulty of every theology is mixed with and dependent upon another difficulty: theology by its very assumption must go beyond the normal area of the applicability of language. Human language was formed through incessant contact with the material world and the world of other people. For that reason our language "normally" functions only in that

126

area. In the meantime, theology is fated to continually go beyond the world of matter and the world of everyday human experiences. If going beyond the range of applicability in physics takes its vengance through paradoxes and antinomies, how much more so must this apply to all attempts to any assertions whatsoever beyond the material world?

Therefore, do the statements of a theologian make any sense whatsoever?

Without doubt, many common utterances seem to change their meaning in a theological context. A trite example: "God is a person". The individual words are understandable to every user of common English; these words are linked together in the sentence in accordance with the grammar of the language completely the same as e.g. in the sentence "John Smith is a person". And, yet, these two sentences do not have the same meaning. What it means to say that John Smith is a person is more or less clear to everyone. What it means to say that God is a person is not clear to even the most brillant theologian.

Precisely here are necessary such theological conceptions as the traditional theory of analogy or the newer theory of the symbolism of theological language (which we shall examine more closely in the next two chapters). They attempt to explain how one can speak in human language about what goes beyond the area of common applications of human language.

Some theologians maintain that, despite all, nothing extra-human can be described in human language: even when a theologian is convinced that he is speaking about transcendence, in reality he is only speaking about the human "reception" of transcendence. These tendencies are called the theological anthropologism (we spoke of them in the second chapter).

These are the difficulties in which each theology is enmeshed: both the theology of the most exquisite masters of this discipline and the theology of the simplest peasant praying at a roadside image.

And, yet, this struggle with the limitations of language is not senseless. Christian Revelation expressed itself in human language, entangling itself in all of its limitations, complications and thicket of meanings, and thereby guaranteeing that, since it was expressed, then it carries meanings, which we should try to understand.

6. Back to the Starting Point.

Here we return to the starting point: the fundamental lack of proportion between the transcendental (from "transcendo" - I am going beyond) content and human means of expression. The present chapter is only an explanation and deepening of what we already said at the very beginning (in the first chapter).

Conflicts which are the result of misunderstanding do exist between reason and faith; misunderstandings should be clarified, and then the conflicts are eliminated. But there are conflicts of a fundamental nature: they result from the essence of human language. These conflicts cannot be eliminated. One must only understand their source; then they cease to disturb us, they become logical. Something in the way of the well-known saying that a recognized necessity becomes freedom.

According to some interpretations of linguistic philosophy, "that which can be conceived can be expressed" in the meaning "that which cannot be expressed cannot be conceived". This is not true. Precisely the deep structure of language wells up from the source where one thinks more than one can say.

Language is an expression of thought. Thought is before the word, but conflicts occur on the level of words, not thoughts. The only way to avoid conflicts would be not to put thoughts into words. But point is that - as Parandowski said - a thought must be expressed, even if only on the cinders of syntax.

Twelve:

The Life of Symbols

> "Everyone knows, for example, that to reproduce a
> word is a relatively simple matter, and words are
> even cheaper than potatoes."
> Alexander Zinoviev, Logic of Science.

> "... all of us moderns are experts in the
> philology of exegesis, the phenomenology of
> religion, psychoanalysis, the analysis of
> language. An so the same epoch forejudges whether
> desolation will occur or whether language will
> again be fulfilled."
> Paul Ricoeur, Symbole donne a penser.

1. Introduction.

Comparison of religious truths with the propositions
of science is shocking. It is not a matter of divergence or
contradiction, but a complete and dramatic dissimilarity. "How
can you believe in these things?" - an astronomer-colleague
once asked me, having earlier provoked a conversation on
religious subjects. An escape from this kind of shocking
comparison often is appeal to the symbolic character of the
language of religion. Is it merely an escape, a subterfuge, or
does it also have some deeper, real justification?

129

Apologists-integralists are afraid of looking for symbolism in religious contents, believing that it threatens truth: what is a symbol can be true only in the same sense as one speaks of "true" poetry. Indeed, in common language the term "symbol" is sometimes associated with such intuitions. But one should remember that if modern theology uses this term, it derives it not from common language, but from the philosophical dictionary. And the term "symbol" has had a dizzying career in contemporary philosophy.

The history of contemporary views on the role of symbols goes back to Freud and Jung. In the hands of psychoanalysts symbol became a key concept leading to an understanding of the states of the human subconsciousness. Eliade constructed a theory of symbol and applied it to an investigation of the history of religion. According to Ricoeur, philosophy should become hermeneutics or the art of interpreting symbols. Structuralism treats symbols as an instrument for making the humanistic sciences more precise, while the importance of symbols in the exact sciences has been long known and requires only rethinking in a new context.

2. Dead Symbols.

Let us begin with exact sciences. The symbolic language of these sciences is known to everyone who at least has encountered elementary algebra. This is a good starting point for discussing symbols in general, though really on the basis of contrast, for everything here is backwards: in the exact sciences the symbol is dead, its meaning remains once and for all frozen in the axioms of a formalized system or in interpretative rules, as far as empirical systems are concerned, whereas in so-called hermeneutic sciences, in religion, in art the meanings of symbols live their own life, changing depending of the content and shades of meaning of other symbols.

The symbols of the formal sciences (mathematics and logic) are "still more dead" than the symbols of the empirical sciences. To be sure, the empirical sciences borrow their symbolic language from mathematics, but in relating it to the data of experience they give it a certain instability: above all, experiments have their own life, are a result of the creative invention of the experimenters - and this cannot be formalized - and, secondly, even the most precisely constructed experiment gives results with a precision only to that of measurement errors. "Experimental data" are not totally convertible into mathematical symbols.

But precisely this "deadness" of symbols appearing in the formal sciences gives them their strength. Behind these symbols are hidden the boldest, purest, most "coldly" invented abstractions which humanity has ever created (1).

The symbols of the formal sciences are also called signs, and the symbolism of these sciences is simply their formalism (2). A formal symbol is the basic unit of a certain formalized language. This language is completely "closed within itself", at no point does it go beyond its own linguistic reality, all meanings are defined by the same "grammar" of the language, without any reference to the "external world" or to our intuition. We can say that the meaning of symbols in formal language is defined in a purely syntactic manner. Knowledge of such a language reduces itself to calculation, or to a certain game with symbols in accordance with the rules that apply in that language.

The language of mathematics, regarded by itself, is empty; it does not relate to the material world, but it can symbolize the relations making up the material world. This statement is not necessary a priori; the entire development of modern science can be regarded as its confirmation. In this statement there is a deep philosophical content. The faith of scientists in the power and truth of mathematics is so absolute that gradually their work to an ever lesser extent is observation and more and more becomes calculation (3).

Analyzed with great subtlety in the methodology of the empirical sciences has been the operation of the so-called interpretation of the formal language through which the enchanted circle of the internal emptiness of this language is broken, imparting empirical meanings to formal symbols (4). However, this is not a simple operation of "linear" subordination; it does not so happen that each "observed datum" receives its one and only one counterpart in the form of some formal symbol. The relation between formalism and reality is much more intimate. Ready information about the world (observed data) does not flow fom experiments; we read the course of events on the screens of oscilloscopes, the indicators of sensitive chronometers, black marks on photographic plates. Already in advance the very mathematized theory of a given instrument suggests to us the proper interpretation. In making use of it, we move bacwards, as it were - again with the assistance of mathematics - from a reading on a scale, through dots on a chart, to something which we are inclined to call an "empirical fact".

What can be directly observed is only a sign of a "physical fact". It requires interpretation to become a scientific assertion. The problem of observation yields to the problem of meaning. And the triumph of empiricism in the exact sciences is threatened by the astonishing truth that our sense data are primarily symbols. (5)

3. Living Symbols.

The interpretation of various kinds of signs is our everyday fate: we react to bells, we observe the hands of a watch, we make gestures and movements: we bow our head, wave our hand, cross the street at the pedestrian crossing, but only when we have a green light, various circles, triangles, pictures of a cigarette with a line trough it, or hands throwing rubbish into a container guide our behavior. Signs can be natural: a wet street and a dry sidewalk is a sign that the street sprinkler has just gone by, smoke from a chimney is a sign that there is a fire in the furnace; or artificial: the raising of a signal disc is a sign for the train to depart, but for a car on a highway a sign to stop.

Signs have meaning only for someone who knows how to interpret them. A certain boy when he came home always rang ten times short and fifteen times long so that his mother would know that it was he. I do not believe that anyone besides the mother would have discovered the key to the correct interpretation of the sign.

There are signs whose meaning function is storied, as it were: the first, direct meaning of the sign refers us - primarily through some analogy - to a second meaning (symbolic) in such a way that the second meaning is not given except through the mediation of the first. The first meaning is somehow transparent, through it one "sees" the second meaning. In a certain sense the first meaning is a sign of the second meaning. Such signs are called symbols. Water is almost natural sign for washing and cleanliness, but under certain circumstances - for example, in some religious ceremonies - this function of the sign-water becomes somehow referred to a new meaning: being washed from sins or spiritual purity.

The meanings of symbols are not established in themselves, nor are they fixed once and for all. They are not established in themselves, but in connection with the meanings of other symbols. They are not fixed once and for all, but have their own life, grow, become enriched or impoverished, and fade with use.

The art of reading the meanings of symbols is called hermeneutics. In the contemporary methodology of the humanistic sciences there is a rich trend emphasizing the role of symbols in these sciences. Hermeneutics would thus be the basic method in these sciences. In this regard, spoken of ever more frequently are the hermeneutic sciences, including among them also philosophy and theology. Supporters of this trend emphasize that, above all, the very language of people is the carrier of symbolic meanings. Of course, a word can be used as a sign – asserts Susanne Langer – but this is not its basic role. A word in itself is a symbol connected with some idea, but not directly with some object or event (6). Language is patterned on thoughts, and thus as far as thoughts are concerned, and on all levels of thought, this is a symbolic process. The essential act of thought is its symbolization (7). In turn the world of thoughts and language is composed within the so-called real world. The real world for man is a world of signs and symbols. A tree, a table, a fork are a tree, table, and fork for man; without man and his ability to assign and read meanings, establish and understand symbols they would be pieces of matter or coils of physical fields, unnamed, not understood, lacking individuality.

Paul Ricoeur in an essay entitled "Symbols Provoke Thought" (8) distinguishes three stages on the way to the understanding of symbol, "three stages – as he writes – marking the way of movement, whose starting point is the life locked within the symbol and point of conclusion the thought conceived based on the symbol".

The first stage consists in placing the symbol in the world of other symbols. So, for example, Ricoeur notes that for Eliade "understanding of the symbol is synonymous with placing it in a certain whole of the same type, but more extensive, creating, a system in the plane to which it belongs".

The second stage consists in applying hermeneutics to the interpretation of symbols: "only within the compass of modern hermeneutics does symbol begin to offer its gift of meaning and the outlines of its deciphering appear".

But this is still not all, the technique alone of manipulating symbols is not enough; the understanding of symbol becomes complete after entering into the third stage, "the stage of thinking going out from the symbol". For it is not a case of juggling with the meanings of symbols, but philosophizing with symbols in order to "solve the riddle of man with the aid of symbols".

4. Symbols and Truth.

Religion thinks in symbols. Each religion, from the most primitive totemisms to the purest theism. If even common language, concerning the most ordinary objects, is entangled with symbols, then how much more so must this be true of pronouncements about what in essence is inexpressible. We began our considerations on the subject of the confrontation reason-faith with the statement of the conflict contained in the very concept of Revelation: a conflict between the content which is to be imparted to man and the conceptual and linguistic apparatus in which this content must be expressed (9). Traditional Christian theology always had a deep feeling of this "lack of proportion" between the content and the form of expression. Thus its statement on the analogous character of all pronouncements about God. For example, if we say "God is just", the word "just" is not synonymous with the same-sounding word appearing in the sentence "John Smith is just". Though, on the other hand, both of these terms are not completely synonymous, they are connected by some similarity of meaning; we say that they are analogous. In this regard, traditional philosophy - as though at the request of theology - formulated the so-called theory of analogy.

The consequence of the analogicalness of our concepts about God - according to traditional philosophy and theology - were three ways of arriving at statements about God: (a) the way of negation: denying to God adjectives implying certain deficiency, imperfection (e.g. when we say that God is non-finite); (b) the way of affirmation: we attribute adjectives to God expressing some perfection (e.g. God is just); and (c) the way of elevation: what we attribute to God positively (by the way of affirmation) we raise to infinite power, as it were. All of these ways of speaking about God (along with the theory of analogy) are an expression of theology's grappling with the necessity of speaking about

That-Which-Completely-Goes-Beyond; and according to modern terminology, they are nothing other than certain hermeneutic rules for attempting to read the symbolic meaning of pronouncements about God.

The awareness of the symbolic nature of the language of theology is a further step in the process of its purification (10); many (if not all) pseudo-dogmas resulted from overlooking the symbolic character of some religious statement or from the use of erroneous hermeneutics. Awareness of the fact that the language of religion is - for it must be - symbolic, on the one hand, sharpens the contrast between the language of faith and the language of the exact sciences in which only "dead symbols" (formal signs) appear, but, on the other hand, softens the drastic dissimilarity of the scientific and religious "picture of the world", and it softens it so effectively that many theologians regard the conflict science-faith as eliminated once and for all.

And yet a disturbing questions remain: Does acquiescence to the symbolic character of the language of religion not threaten its truth? Do symbolic readings of religious documents (e.g. the Bible) not undermine the historicalness of events of fundamental significance for religion? I believe that these questions arise from a certain ambiguity. For many people the common statement "this has symbolic meaning" means that "this" should be understood as a metaphor, not literally, while the word "symbol" becomes the opposite of literalness, truth, history. In speaking of the symbolic nature of the language of religion we do not have in mind common associations of this sort, but we use the term "symbol" in the meaning formulated by modern philosophy (presented in the third section of this chapter). In this meaning symbol does not have to oppose history; for an understanding of history one simply has to apply hermeneutcs (history is a hermeneutic science). Through symbolic thinking truth is not eliminated, but is made closer. (11)

Thirteen:

The Conflict of Two Languages

1. Introductory Remarks.

Among the many Western publications on the subject "science and faith" I took note of the small book by Ferdinand Chapey "Science et foi - affrontement de deux langages" (Science and Faith - Confrontation of Two Languages) (1). It differs from the others in the boldness of its thought and radicalness of its considerations. Despite a certain one-sidedness, it seems to me that this book should not be too quickly returned to the shelf after it has been read.

What is the one-sidedness at issue? In the problem science and faith two sides are involved: science and faith. Chapey's book is one-sided in the sense that it can be "trusted" only in the theological sense. To be sure, the author does not make errors when he writes of the problem of science (which often happens to other author-theologians), but one can sense that he does not move with complete freedom over areas reserved to science. So, for example, as the leading problem of science of the twentieth century - which earlier was mechanics or evolutionism - the author regards the "development of the biosphere into the noosphere". Here one can see more the influence of Teilhard de Chardin than modern science.

In Chapey's opinion, the fundamental divergence between the "scientific mentality" and the "mentality of faith" is that science runs into the future, while faith is rooted in the past. On page 18 we read the somewhat pathetic statement: "More than at any other time science is identified with the destiny of mankind. It is humanity on the march. The scientist has an awareness of participating in this march". On the other hand, believing man looks backward (this should not necessarily be understood in the pejorative sense). Even if faith refers to future things (eschatology), it has its justification in the past. The scientist and the theologian do not look in the same direction. But what happens when the scientist and theologian (believing man) are the same person? A certain kind of internal rupture takes place which is the psychological source of the whole problem.

The problem swells still further if its social dimensions are considered. In a very short period of time scientific methods have not only developed tremendously, but they have also become a research tool in the hands of an ever growing number of people. Neither can it be forgotten that science also exerts a strong influence outside the circle of scientists alone. In the eyes of the masses it has acquired nearly unshakable authority. This authority is so universal that Chapey does not hesitate to say that "humanity in its planetary dimensions for the first time has a common language", the language of science.

One might question whether the most essential divergence between science and religion is a different perspective of looking, forward and backward, but it is indisputable that the conflict today has reached "planetary dimensions".

Despite its debatableness - or perhaps precisely because of it - Chapey's book is thought-provoking. And this is its great value.

2. The Methodology of the Dispute.

It is obvious that none of the parties at variance - given any sort of law-abidingness - can be the judge of the dispute. Besides, from the moment when a scientist begins to ask questions about the limits and value of scientific cognition, he ceases to be a scientist and becomes a philosopher of science. Similarly, a theologian posing the problem of the value and sense of religious cognition enters into the area of the philosophy of religion. According to Chapey, philosophy (of science and of religion) is the proper ground on which to state and examine the problem of science and faith.

The author stipulates that by philosophy he does not understand some superscience which would authoritatively enter into all gaps in our knowledge. Modern philosophy reserves a much more modest role for itself. Its essential task is not so much to find answers as to pose questions: reflection and invitation to reflection. Above all, reflection on the significance of human actions and human consciousness.

This last formulation anounces that Chapey understands philosophy in the spirit of Husserl. For him the philosophy of science identifies with the phenomenology of science, and the philosophy of religion with the phenomenology of religion. The first chapter of his book ("Une methode de reflexion") is an able introduction to the method of phemomenological analysis.

Here my most serious objections arise. I believe that Husserl's phenomenology is just as alien to the "scientific mentality" as theology itself and if for only this reason is not very suited to be an arbiter in the dispute between science and faith. The introduction of a "third side" to the dispute as an arbiter, about whom at best people of science say they are unable to understand, can only still further complicate the situation. Nevertheless, I regard the conclusions of Chapey's analysis as interesting. I suspect that they could have been achieved – and even in a more natural manner – without the use of the methods of phenomenology.

3. The Essence of Science.

What is the essence of the "scientific attitude"? Let us seek the answer through the process of elimination. Firstly, then, what is it not? And so, in the first place, "reality" or also the "objective world", about which science allegedly speaks, does not enter into this essence. From the times of Kant it has been known that "things-in-themselves" are not directly accessible to cognition; here the issue is the same. Secondly, the essence of science is not a collection of information acquired and stored by science nor – thirdly – even less so a "vision of the world" constructed on the basis of this information. The information acquired by science is a very important element of science , determining its power and importance for culture, but – in the opinion of the author – it is not this that gives science its "sense". To an even greater extent this concerns so-called scientific visions of the world. Such a vision of the world in the nineteenth century was mechanism or total evolutionism. They are rather by-products of science, "scientific myths" always treated with great suspicion by non-philosopher scientists.

Every phenomenon investigated by science is dependent on other phenomena, and these in turn on still others, etc. Science "breaks down" these regressions and expresses them – insofar as possible – in the form of mathematical functions. Scientific explanation always takes the form of a conditional statement: "if ..., then ...". If a set of such and such conditions appears, then these and these phenomena follow. The set of conditions of a given phemomenon forms a certain structure; this structure has its conditioning in structures of higher order, and so on. Scientific explanation never closes, never reaches the "unconditional level".

The language of mathematics is best suited to express conditionality. As is known, it is constructed from "pure relations". Mathematics is not interested in the elements among which the relations occur, but only in the "relational web" itself. And the relational web is nothing other than the system of conditionings. For that reason the language of mathematics is the language of the empirical sciences. Conditionality is the essence of the "scientific consciousness". The truth of science – Chapey emphasizes – is always conditional truth.

4. The Essence and Language of Religion.

What, in turn, does the "phenomenon of religion" consist in? The matter does not concern submitting one or another religion to analysis either from the aspect of its doctrinal content or in its historical context or from any other point of view. The matter concerns grasping the very essence of "religious consciousness". The chapter "L'essence de la religion" is an elementary but – one must admit – a very lucid presentation of the conclusions of the so-called phenomenology of religion.

In order to get to its very essence phenomenology "takes religion in parentheses" (Husserl's expression) or at a given stage of its considerations excludes from them everything which is not its essence. And thus, firstly, for the moment we are not interested in the truth of religious statements. In no sense is this a declaration in favor of atheism or even skepticism. We simply wish to look for the essence of "religious consciousness" without taking up the problem of the truth of the assertions of any concrete religion. Secondly, we put aside analyses concerning various empirical aspects of the study of religion; such as: the fact of the existence of a multitude of various religions, their dogmatic assertions, practices and religious institutions, etc. Thirdly, we exclude from our present investigations various theories of religion; e.g. the theory stating that religion performs only the function of integrating society (Durkheim), the theory according to which religion is the ideology of ruling class at a certain stage in the development of society (Marx), the theory alleging that religions arose from fear and desire (Freud), and others.

After such a "reduction" what is left of religion? Religiosity in the pure state, the very essence of the religious consciousness? It is - according to phemomenologists - UNCONDITIONAL experience, experience which encompasses the WHOLE man. Precisely these two elements: unconditionality and totality. Let us attempt to remove either one of them. Immediately the phenomenon of religion disappears and, at most one of its substitutes remains.

Human language in all of its aspects is marked by limitations and conditionings. How, then, can one speak of the Unconditional? All human pronouncements bear the stamp of fragmentariness. How can one express what embraces everything? As we have seen in the previous chapter modern theology emphasizes the symbolic nature of the language of belief. Symbols somehow burst all ordinary linguistic frames: they are rooted in language, but by their designative function they extend to extralinguistic reality, which is directly inexpressible. The symbol makes present something which is not contained in itself. One can speak of the Inexpressible only in the language of symbols.

We once more strongly emphasize - the symbolic nature of some language is not a sign of its illusoriness . The symbol can olso carry a load of truth (or falsity). This is only truth, as it were, of "another kind" (e.g. the truth of a poem differs "qualitatively" from the truth of a history textbook). The religious symbol refers us to Inexpressible Reality, but very often it also somehow works in the oppposite direction - evokes the presence of the Inexpressible in the symbolic gesture or word. Revelation today is apprehended not as much as the communication to people of a certain collection of information, but as the realization of that which is professed. Let us leave the subtlety of these problem to theologians.

5. Confrontation of Languages.

Focusing on the symbolic nature of the language of religion is the key to resolve the conflict between science and faith. The language of science tries to express the mutual conditionings of phenomena in the form of mathematical relationships. The language of religion through symbol strives to grasp the Unconditioned One and complete involvement in Him. If the language of faith speaks of finite reality, then very often - so as not to use always - it treats it as a symbol of the Infinite One.

In the opinion of contemporary theologians, awareness of these linguistic differentiations in principle eliminates all conflicts between science and religion. The languages of science and religion, though they ostensibly speak about the same thing, refer to completely different aspects of reality. Thus they are, in their essence, not in conflict. Moreover, Chapey stresses that - contrary to a rather widespread opinion - the languages of science and faith are not even complementary. Religion in no way is a complement to that which science has not yet discovered, while science, because of the essential limitations of its method, remains completely helpless in the field of religion. For that reason all possible conflicts can only be a misunderstanding, such or another misdirection of linguistic competencies.

The distinction of two "lingustic orders" is relatively simple and almost suggests itself. Why, then, do conflicts between science and religion still continue to exist and still disturb so many people? Historically speaking, the philosophy of language (on whose achievements the above analysis are at bottom based) is relatively young and its conclusions not well known outside a circle of specialists. Furthermore, all too often so-called "scientific myths" are taken for science itself. Scientific myths are a certain interpretation of the conclusions (or methods) of science, usually consisting in extreme generalizations. These myths not infrequently play the role of a "substitute religious creed" (Rahner) and then they can be in conflict or - contrariwise - "scientifically" justify one religion or another. An example of the "atheistic myth" is materialistic evolutionism, a "spiritualistic myth" - Teilhardism. These are two - going in opposite directions - philosophical generalizations of the scientific theory of evolution, which in itself is philosophically (as a world outlook) neutral. In fact it never comes to a conflict between science and faith, only between a scientist and a believer (even if they happen to be the same person), between some scientific myth of the former and religious convictions of the latter.

In the last chapter of his book Chapey emphasizes the purifying role which science performs in relation to religion (2). Without the conflict with science it probably would never have become aware of the symbolic component of its language. The confrontation with science cleanses religion of "theological myths". Hence an important lesson for theologians: despite the diversity of linguistic planes, close contacts with the science should be maintained. It would be naive to believe that the purification process of theology has been completed.

But in the opinion of Chapey and many other theologians the differentiation of "linguistic orders" eliminates the essence of the dispute. Psychological reasons remain. Symbolic language does not speak to modern man, who wishes everything to be said simply and unambiguously. This tendency surely stems from the spirit of science and technics, where the principle of maximum economy in the means of expression is in force. Everything points to the fact that the so-called conflict between science and faith will long remain a burning issue of wide social dimensions.

6. Critical Remarks.

In many respects Chapey's book is symptomatic. The conflict science-faith has all but ceased to be a conflict for theologians. It is quite natural that precisely theologians had to be the first to grapple with this problem. After all, it threatened their very reason for existence. Unfortunately, the consideration of the problem matured in theological analyses and reflections with practically no dialogue with scientists. It turns out that division between the world of theologians and the world of science is not less - and certainly more visible - than between the language of science and faith. In effect, correct results of theological analyses often remain completely unknown to people from scientific circles. And not only because of a lack of interest. The language of theological treatises - including those intended for popular consumption - is too hermetic, even in those parts which have nothing to do with symbolism.

Chapey's book is an example. I doubt whether the average reader with a so-called scientific mentality would successfully plow through the greater part of his deliberations (and Chapey clearly aims at popularization). Use

143

of the methods of Husserl's phenomenology certainly does not contribute to an improvement of this situation. So, for example, it seems to me that the concept "essence of scientific consciousness" for many scientists remains rather clouded. Would it not be simpler to say that the feature of the "conditionality" of scientific cognition is essential for our considerations? It is possible to demonstrate the existence of this feature - in a more natural and effective way than with phenomenological methods - with the aid of the ordinary philosophy of science. After all, the philosophy of science is the most suitable court for investigating the sciences, their methods, area of competencies, etc. And - which is very important for practical reasons - the language of the philosophy of science is ever more respected by people actively engaged in science.

Finally, a summing-up question: is the symbolism of the language of religion an all-purpose anti-conflict remedy? Examination of the arguments performed above convincingly shows that the distinction of "linguistic planes" has a real basis in the structure of both languages. The present analyses of theologians are certainly a big step forward, but it is hard to believe that the problem has been closed once and for all. A conflict situation will remain if only for the reason that various "linguistic levels" encounter each other in the mind of one person: the believing scientist, the theologian who does not isolate himself from the attainments of modern science, the educated man who is concerned with the development of his own general and religious culture. Every mind strives toward synthesis, or at least only a symbiosis, of its views, even if they come from different drawers.

Recapitulation

The history of modern physics provides us with a lesson whose importance goes far beyond the field of physical applications. For nearly three centuries Newtonian mechanics was regarded as the fundamental science of reality (mechanism). Its replacement, at the beginning of our century, by relativistic mechanics and quantum mechanics teaches us to be wary of too hasty generalizations. Our intellectual constructions as a rule have a limited area of applicability. What might seem a general regularity usually does not apply beyond a certain limit.

The same concerns language. We speak in common language about fields which we control by everyday experience. But outside these fields common language may already no longer be suited to transmit information. Modern philosophy of science again gives us a warning. Classical mechanics uses "stylized" common language, but this language ceases to be adequate in quantum mechanics. For example, concepts so fundamental for the "ontology" of common language as the concept of the individuality of particles and their localization lose their ordinary meaning in quantum mechanics.

Human cognition is zonal: it does not embrace all of reality, but only a certain limited area of it and not from all possible points of view, but only from one certain narrowed point of view. This zonalness of cognition reflects itself on language. Language shaped in one "zone" in principle expresses nothing when it is mechanically transferred to another "zone".

The superficial level of language can be learned from grammars and dictionaries, the deep level of language can be learned only by using it (language games). The deep structure of common language is determined by the conditions in which this language is used. The majority of conflicts in daily life arise from the fact that for the sides in the dispute the language used has the same superficial level, but completely different deep levels (game conflicts).

All of these difficulties are increased in the field of religion and theology. Religious language developed on the basis of common language, but the language of religion (and theology) is fated to incessantly go beyond the material world, and hence beyond the world of ordinary. human experiences. Theo-religious language is based on common language, but in contradistinction to the latter is lacking the interpretation of its deep structure in the everyday activities of man.

There exist conflicts between religion and science which result from misunderstanding; these can and should be eliminated. But there also exist conflicts between religion and science which stem from the essence of human language. These conflicts cannot be eliminated. One must simply understand their source.

One of the efforts to understand the essence of the language of faith is to note its symbolic character. The concept of symbol is being made precise by modern philosophy. I emphasize - the matter here does not concern symbol in the common meaning, but that understanding of symbol as is used in present day philosophy (e.g. Ricoeur) and following it by theology. (I encourage the Reader to thoroughly assimilate the concept of symbol; to this end one should carefully study chapter 12.) In particular, the symbolic nature of some pronouncement does not negate its truthfulness.

If common speech, language about the most everyday objects, is entangled in symbols, how much more so is this the case with the language of religion (and theology). It appears that only through symbols can human language rise to express the Inexpressible. This is not synonymous with denying the truth of religion; it simply means that for a proper understanding of the language of faith the use of hermeneutics, or the art of understanding symbols, is indispensable.

Awareness of the symbolic nature of the language of religion mitigates the conflict between religion and science, and in the opinion of many theologians from the outset eliminates the possibility of any conflicts whatsoever. The horizons, but also cast new light on already known facts. History has often recorded that conquerors have submitted to the culture of their subjects. And this was generally to the conquerors' benefit. The rationality of conquest will surely be different from its positivistic ideal (13).

A religious conviction without committal is lifeless and is only a hair's breadth away from hypocrisy. Committal to religion without conviction is hung in mid-air and requires a constant effort not to ask the question why one is committed.

5

TOWARD A SYNTHESIS

The analyses made on the previous pages have shown the distinctness of religion and science. I do not intend to question this conclusion. Understanding this distinctness is essential for forming a proper view on the problem of the mutual relations between religion and science. However, there is something that connects these two fields of man's activity. First, both religion (faith) and science (knowledge) are specific kinds of cognition, ways of approaching truth. And truth is one - as is often said. Second, both religion and science belong to the field of human activity. Man attempts to harmonize various elements in himself, even though they might come from methodologically very remote sources. Understanding the diversity of cognition through faith and cognition through science makes possible their symbiosis, but man aims at a synthesis of his views.

The first chapter of this part (chapter 14) takes up the problem of faith. Can the concept of involvement replace the concept of truth in religion? Without involvement there is no authentic religiosity, but can religiosity be authentic if it is not true, i, e. if it does not claim that its assertions are true?

The next chapter (chapter 15) directly poses the problem of synthesis. Human cognition is stratified, strata can become isolated, coming from science, philosophy, religion and other "unorganized" fields. In these considerations we are, above all, interested in the "scientific stratum" and "religious stratum". How are both of these strata arranged in the mind of modern man? Do prospects exist for a true synthesis?

Both chapters came into being from reflections on readings: chapter fourteen from reflections on Roger Trigg's book "Reason and Commitment". Chapter fifteen from looking backwards on considerations made in all of the previous chapters.

Fourteen:

Pilate's Question

Everyone who is of truth hears my voice. Pilate
spoke unto him: What is truth? Having said this
he departed ..."

John 18:37-38.

1. From Truth to Efficiency.

The opportunity to write this chapter was presented to
me by Roger Trigg's book "Reason and Commitments" (1). I do
not intend to write either a review or a paraphrase of it; I
only desire to formulate certain thoughts which probably even
at that - though perhaps slightly differently - would have
been formulated without the help of professor Trigg, since
they are indispensable to the totality of considerations on
the problem science-faith.

For long centuries the striving for truth has been
regarded as the goal of any more organized investigative
reflections. Very often the word "Truth" is written with a
capital T, thereby expressing respect for the goal of the
intellectual task. A philosopher is - by definition - a
searcher and lover of wisdom. Descartes in his "Discourse on
Method" confesses: "I do not cease to feel the greatest
satisfaction with the advances which, I believe, I have
already made in searching for truth ... If among purely human
occupations is found even one genuinely valuable and

151

important, it will be exactly the one I have chosen". Later
scholar-scientists joined philosophers. I believe that even
today many passers-by questioned on the street would answer
that the task of science is to discover truth. But what is
truth? Philosophers very quickly directed this Pilate-like
question at the empirical sciences and at themselves. The
question of Pilate was not a question in the hope of receiving
an answer, it was a calling into question. Already Comte
degraded the role of scientific cognition to the making of
successful predictions. The Comptian "to know in order to
predict" (savoir pour prevoir) suddenly changed into "to know
in order to act". Today it has become very fashionable - this
is perhaps an echo of post-positivistic tradition - to ascribe
purely practical goals to science. Science exists in order to
give man power.

If the word "truth" is disappearing from scientific
implied meaning, then what can we say about religion? If the
empirical method, which somehow menages to touch reality,
seems to be resigning from pretensions to the truth of its
assertions, replacing them with the ambition for effective
action, then how shall we treat the religion, which, after all
concerns untouchable reality? However, it turns out that even
with respect to religion one can speak of a certain kind of
efficiency: religion is efficient if it influences the life of
the believer. Involvement in religion is something essential,
for without involvement there is no true religiosity. Sometimes
- often with the best apologistic intentions - one goes still
further: the concept of involvement begins to displace the
concept of veracity. And then the criterion of meaningfulness
of religious statements becomes the degree of involvement in
them. A peculiar reductionism: the whole of religion is
reduced to human actions.

2. Did Wittgenstein Believe in the Last Judgment?

At the beginning of the modern philosophy of language
stood Ludwig Wittgenstein, from the period of "Philosophical
Investigations" (2). Also having their beginning with him are
views absolutizing the role of religious involvement.
We illustrate Wittgenstein's position by an example
taken from his "Lectures and Conversations on Aesthetics,
Psychology and Religious Belief" (3). Above all, religious
conviction differs very essentially from other human

convictions, especially from persuasions acquired by way of
science. Let us assume - says Wittgenstein - that someone
bases his life on belief in the Last Judgment. He has always
this before his eyes. On what basis can one acknowledge that
he believes in that or not? To ask him would not be enough.
Probably he would assert that he has a proof. However, the
proof would not be appealing to the usual methods of
validating opinions, but rather it would consist in a kind of
the influence on the arrangement of his whole life. This is
what should be called involvement. This way of believing should
be recognized as the strongest of all, since it inclines one
to take a risk such as one would never take for other motives
of which one knows that they are much better founded.

The question arises: can one transmit to someone the
content of one's belief in the Last Judgment as one, for
example, transmits knowledge of quantum mechanics?
Wittgenstein asks himself if he understands the content of
belief in the last Judgment, and he answers: I understand, in
a sense, everything he says, the English words "God",
"judgment", etc. I could even say "I do not believe in that".
And this would be true in the sense that I have no such
thoughts. However, I could not deny it. My usual technique of
using language is not adequate here.

The last sentence is the key to understanding of
Wittgenstein. The problem of the veracity of language reduces
itself to the technique of its use. The technique of the
"language game" is defined by the "ways of life" of the users
of that language (4). The way of life defining the religious
language game is involvement. Involvement defines the meaning of
religious pronouncements. Without involvement religious
language means nothing, it is empty.

Wittgenstein does not combat religious belief; he does
not assert that what the religious person believes in has no
meaning at all. Religious judgements are meaningless to the
non-believer, since, being non-involved, he has no measure of
the sense of religious pronouncements; but for the believer
religious judgements have meaning, his involvement designates
their meaning for him. One cannot carry over models of
meaningfulness from one language to another, e.g. from secular
language to religious language. That running with the ball
under one's arm is a violation of the rules of soccer does not
mean that the rugby player commits an infraction when he does
the same. This figurative comparison can be understood almost

153

literally: language has the status of a game, just like soccer
or rugby.

3. How to Convert Wittgenstein?

Roger Trigg regards Wittgenstein's views as dangerous
for religious belief, since they lead in a straight line to
subjectivism and relativism: what is true for one can be false
for another; what is valid for a certain social group can be
invalid for another group. Everything depends upon who is
involved in what and how. In these conditions concepts do not
depend of the structure of the world, but define this
structure. Various concepts point to various worlds, and so
which world appears is dependent on the conceptual system and
the language of that system.

Trigg considers such a position not only as contrary
to common sense, but also as entangling itself in its own
contradictions and leading astray any more serious religious
thinking. The assertion that God created the world - he says
not without irony - is almost a tautology in the eyes of a
Christian, but obviously human involvement in God does not
create the world. In Trigg's opinion there is a court of
appeal from all the intricacies and entanglements of language;
is its truth. For that reason pronouncements - religious ones
as well - can simply be true or false, irregardless of
someone's involvment in them. Furthermore, belief in their
veracity is a necessary condition of involvment. Committals
contain claims to truth, logically prior to committals.

Hence only Wittgenstein placed head-over-heels can be
a believing Wittgenstein.

However, there is still another way of converting
Wittgenstein. It was undertaken by Agnes Lagache in the book
"Wittgenstein - La logique d'un Dieu" (5). She basically
accepts Wittgenstein's views on language. The meanings carried
by language are qualified by the modes of life, or in the case
of religious pronouncements by committments, while "what we
cannot speak about we must pass over in silence" (6). For that
reason I cannot speak about God to someone who is not
committed, or is involved differently from me. Traditional
Christian philosophy already knew that one cannot meaningfully
speak with words about God. But "that which cannot be spoken
of can be indicated" (7). The silence of the language about
God is a sign or symbol pointing to God.

In this way we have a deeply - though perhaps "anonimously" - believing Wittgenstein. One can interpret thesis 6.41 of the "Tractatus" in this spirit: "The sense of the world must lie outside the world. ... If there is any value that does have value, it must lie outside the whole sphere of what happens and is the case". Or even more clearly in his "Notebooks":

"I know that the world exist ...
That something puzzling exists in it
which we call its sense. ...
The meaning of life,
and thus the meaning of the world
can be given the name God ..." (8)

However, the personal views of Wittgenstein are ultimately not so important, what is essential is the problem itself: in what sense can one speak of the veracity of religious beliefs? (9)

4. Rational Faith.

So let us return to the question: is committal the sole yardstick of the sense of religious pronouncements? An affirmative answer is based on the same assumptions as the neopositivistic belief that the sense of any statement whatsoever is its verifiability. In the case of scientific statements the matter concerns empirical verifiability, while in the case of religious pronouncements committment performs the role of verifiability. Meanwhile, I am firmly convinced - contrary to all kinds of positivism - that meaning and verifiability are conceptually two different things. Of course, one can make them identical through definition, but this would be a definition inconsistent with the common - but in this case completely warranted - understanding of these terms. In order to decide whether some statement is verifiable, I must understand first what it meanings is. A condition of rational committal in something is first apprehending the content of that something.

Here we come to the core of the problem. Religious belief must be rational, i.e. it must be based on sensible reasons. Obviously, the rationality of religious belief is different from the rationality of scientific beliefs. How different? All of the analyses made in this book aim at finding the answer to this question. Rationality cannot be abandoned. Irrational faith would have to remain in irreconcilable conflict with science. And in each case this conflict would be fatal to irrational faith. Trigg is right when he says that the possibility of rationality is such a basic assumption that it seems that when we negate it there remains rationally very little left to say. Rationality is such a fundamental postulate that paradoxically one can say that blindly, without giving any reasons whatsoever, one can become committed only to rationality.

Another important question ineluctably looms: what is, and what is based on, the rationality of religious beliefs? For the moment we leave this intriguing question without answer. It seems to me that the answer to it is part of that personal effort that each person must make in laying out his own path to rational faith.

In any case, rationality is closely connected with truth. And again, truth is not the same thing as verifiability or committal (which should be regarded as a certain kind of test of that which we are committed to). For example, truth of the crime is independent of the verdict of the jury. The acquittal of a murderer cannot restore life to his victim.

An essential function of language is to transmit what we recognize as truth. But truth itself cannot be reduced solely to interlinguistic manipulations. Using a comparison of Whitehead, truth is to language as great literature is to particular words and grammar rules.

Finally, problems of truth are not eliminated even from philosophy of science. To be convinced of this it is worth reading Popper's book "Objective Knowledge". Popper did not hesitate to write: "Our main concern in philosophy and science should be the search for truth" (11), and after two hundred and several dozen pages he repeats the same thing in almost identical phrasing (12). Each time this simple statement is followed by intricate analyses to validate it. The point is that what is true need hardly be obvious.

The question of Pilate is not simple. What is truth? In order to clear up this question mark one would have to write a thick volume. Besides, that is not indispensable. Truth is such that instead of defining it one can strive towards it. And precisely this is committal.

5. Committal.

Does it mean that I entirely agree with Trigg? Not completely. Trigg exaggerates on the other side when he contends that in reality religious convictions do not differ unduly from other convictions as far as their relation to action is concerned. The main difference lies in their subject; religious convictions concern that which is regarded as momentous (12). What does it mean that they do not differ "unduly"? It is true that the difference lies in the subject-matter, but it is precisely the specificity of the subject-matter that influences action and to such an extent that the difference between religious convictions and other kinds of convictions becomes really significant. This difference appears immediately when we compare the reserved certainty of a mathematician who has reached a sought for solution with the determination of a man who tied his entire life, all of his longing for happiness, to belief in the Highest Value. This determination cannot be reserved (though it is very rarely accompanied by any flights of imagination), it is precisely committal. A mathematical discovery is external to the mathematician; religious faith absorbs the believer. Wittgenstein understood this well: "such a way of believing must be recognized as the most powerful of all, since it inclines man to take risk which he would not take for other things".

Of course, religious convictions can be studied on a plane equal to that of other convictions (some analytical philosophers do this), but thereby they so falsify them that they cease to be themselves. This is perhaps an even greater falsification than the killing of a living cell and placing it under a microscope in order to discover the essence of life.

But the fact that the committal enters into the very core of a religious conviction cannot disparage the rationality of that conviction. Rational reasons should precede committal. Committal itself must also be rational.

Of course, this is possible only under the condition of not equating the field of rationality with the field controlled by the empirical sciences. Rationality betrays itself if, instead of expanding the area of its influences, it submits to the temptation of safely keeping within the home confines of empiricism. However, one must also be prepared for the eventuality that leaving the turnpike can not only expand language of science attempts to express the mutual conditioning of phenomena in the form of mathematical functions. The pronouncements of religion in constant struggle with the inertia of human language attempt to express the Inexpressible and our complete involvement in it. If the language of faith speaks of finite reality, then it (always?) treats it as a symbol of the Infinite.

But differentiating the zones (or levels) of cognition and indicating the distinctness of the languages of religion and science do not completely solve the problem, if only for the reason that various zones and various languages strive for synthesis or at least a symbiosis of views, even if they are derived from sources that are methodologically completely distinct.

Fifteen:

From Symbiosis to Synthesis

1. What Does Science Give Faith?

What does modern science give to religious faith? After the considerations that have been made up to the present such a question may seem out of place. After all, in previous chapters we showed clearly enough - as I beleve - the basic dissimilarity in the range of interests, methods of approach, nature of cognition, means of expression, language and goals of science and faith. If we are inclined to simultaneously grant the right of existence to religion and science, then it is on the basis of a strict division of competencies and non-interference in the internal matters of the former opponent. However, the modern science has certain characteristics which enable the man of today who is in contact with it to more easily believe than, for example, his predecessor one hundred years ago. Flowing from these characteristics are: the feeling of limitations of our knowledge and the feeling that we are participating in something that surpasses us.

It is obvious that these "feelings" do not automatically result from contact with science at the pressing of a button. There are people who have opposite feelings, but I would insist that they do not belong among those who are the most intimately familiar with the spirit of modern science. What is called the modern scientific climate does not breed conceit.

2. The Feeling of Limitation.

The feeling of the limitation of knowledge today has a variety of faces. Beginning with the simplest: modern physics in contradistinction to the so-called classical physics knows two constants that limit - one from below and the other from above - our invesigative horizon. Planck's constant places barrier on the preciseness of measurements. For example, one cannot simulataneously and to any degree of precision determine the location and momentum of an electron. The indeterminacy of measurement cannot be reduced indefinitely. It has a granular structure: indeterminacy cannot be less than permitted by Planck's constsnt. The world below Planckian dimensions is inaccessible to our measurements.

The second "limiting constant" is the speed of light in a vacuum. This is the maximum and unpassable speed of transmitting information in nature. The situation is not saved even by greatly hypothetical tachyons, particles moving with speeds greater than that of light, since they in turn - if they exist at all - cannot surpass the speed of light from below (they cannot slow down to or below the speed of light). In one way or another the speed of light in a vaccum is the absolute barrier for the flow of information that we can send or receive.

Because of the existence of a maximum speed for the flow of information not all of space-time is accessible to the investigations of the earthly observer. There are regions of space-time from which we can receive light signals (information); there are also regions in space-time to which we can send light signals and such regions of space-time to which we can neither send nor from which we can receive any signals whatsoever. The barrier is precisely the speed of light; in order to reach these inaccessible regions we would have to have at our disposal signals which move faster than light, and there are no such in nature. This kind of limitation of the regions of space-time accessible to our investigative exploration would hold true even if it turned out that the Universe in which we live is infinite in space.

There is still another powerful limitation to our possible investigations. Modern cosmology asserts that the presently unfolding evolution of the Universe began from what is called an initial singular state. The singularity of this state is based on the fact that if we move back in time toward the initial singularity, the volume of the Universe shrinks to zero, while the density of matter contained in the Universe grows to infinity. Initial singularity is also metaphorically called the Big Bang, since it sent into motion the flight of the galaxies or the expansion of the Universe. The essential feature of initial singularity is that it is a hermetic membrane for information concerning periods "before" the singularity. The word "before" is put in quotation marks in order to point out that we do not know whether there even were some "pre-singularity states". Metaphorically one can say that if the Universe existed before the singularity, then it has forgotten what it was like (1).

In some models of the Universe besides the initial singularity there is also a final singularity. It is then also a hermetic membrane for information to that which will be - if anything will still exist - "after" it (2).

However, not only the existence of these "informational thresholds" (Planck's constant from below, the speed of light from above and cosmological singularities "from the beginning and from the end") make a scientist aware of the feeling of the limitation of his knowledge. Above all, the matter here concerns a certain disproportion between what becomes known and what still remains to be known, a fact which is felt in the struggle with even the most insignificant scientific problem: each riddle captured from nature results in a chain reaction of successive riddles, and the solution of the following riddles in this continual avalanche requires ever more subtle research methods and, inexonerably, ever greater investments of time, money, and organization. Can this go on without end?

3. The Feeling of Participation.

All of these results in the fact that the researcher hardly feels himself to be a wise teacher who puts test questions to nature and receives answers: "That is right, professor" or more rarely: "I'm sorry, this time you are wrong". The readers of cheap science-fiction stories could imagine such situations. Scintific research is not the asking of examination questions of nature but is - as I have said - participation and a twofold participation at that: in the process of the development of science and in something that surpasses this development, while simultaneously making it possible at all, what we commonly call reality.

There is a rich literature on the theories of the development of science. Various trends are represented in it: from "The Logic of Scientific Discovery" of Popper to "The Structure of Scientific Revolutions" of Kuhn. Does science develop through the accumulation of achievements or, on the contary, is the essence of science to continually reassess its own foundations and incessantly question its results? All of the possible combinations of these two opposite formulations can also be taken into consideration, and many examples from the history of science are cited in support of them. In one way or another the position of the "logicians" is correct in the sense that the development of science - irregardless of whether this development is understood as linear growth or as successively overturned scientific regimes - certain internal logical laws are in command. Even individuals of genius cannot repeal these laws. If scientific genius consists in going outside the limits of ordinariness, then the ordinary limits of scientific development (precisely this "inner logic" of science) work in such a way as to give geniuses specified places in the space of scientific discoveries. Both the genius as well as the rank-and-file scientific worker are cogs, wheels, and transmission belts of the great machine. To be sure, this machine is not run by the laws of classical mechanics, which from a knowledge of the present state of the machinery would enable one to open up its entire past and future history; nonetheless, the "inner logic" of science exists and governs the elements of the entire construction in the name of the interests of the whole which in this case is certainly not equivalent to the sum of its parts.

The development of science surpasses the individuals who created this development.

If the development of science - metaphorically speaking - is greater than the sum of the individuals creating it, then what is this "surplus"? The sum of the efforts of many researchers scattered throughout the entire world moves toward SOMETHING. This Something reveals its various faces under the condition that it is compelled to do so by a properly posed question and by a method allowing the flow of information from this Something to the researcher. This Something is commonly called REALITY. The researcher himself belongs to it and participates in its realness.

The cultivation of science very often affords similar experiences.

4. Symbiosis - Stratification.

An unmistakable conclusion of the considerations of the previous chapters is the statement that there exists - by mutual agreement we shall call it - a stratification of planes

162

which in great simplification one can represent with the aid
of the following schema:

Mathematicized	(speculation)	Revelation
experience	(philosophy)	theology
the sciences		

I have bracketed the middle elements of this schema
since our considerations solely concern the relations between
science and religion, and I have no intention of confusing the
matter by getting involved in discussions and polemics
concerning philosophy and its scientific status.

The afore-mentioned stratification of planes makes
possible the symbiosis of religious faith with contemporary
scientifc thought. The division of competencies and
non-interference in the internal affairs of the partner is a
condition for peaceful co-existence.

A disturbing question arises: is this stratification
of planes, the admission of the lack of competency in the
affairs of the previous opponent not just a tactical
manoeuvre, a temporary concession for the price of which one
can obtain clear benefits?

The expression "aspectness" does not sound too well in
English, but I could not find any other expression for this
feature of human cognition due to which our mind is unable to
devote itself to the contemplation (in the broadest meaning of
this word) of several things at the same time. When some
object finds itself in the center of attention, the contours
of all the others become blurred on the edges of the field of
consciousness. If we wish to investigate the course of many
variables, we successively have to "freeze" all of the
variables with the exception of one, and in this manner
reconstruct the evolution of the entire structure. (The reader
who is familiar with the so-called partial differentiation in
mathematics knows exactly what I have in mind).

I am inclined to believe - the reader will forgive me
this metaphysical digression, which is really not essential to
the whole of our considerations - that this sort of aspectlike
selectiveness of our mind results from the fact that it is
fated to operate in one-dimensional time. The model of
one-dimensionality is a straight line. Events occurring in our
mind follow one after another like points along a line and in
this way we get the feeling of the one-dimensionality of time.
The line of time cannot either branch out or change into
plane; there is no place on the line for two simultaneous
events, one event has to follow another; our mind cannot deal

with two things at the same time. It is strictly
one-aspectlike, since it is fused with time.

The one-aspectness of our mind has carried over to our
cognition as a whole. A stratification of our view on the
world has taken place. And here again the concept of time
played an important role. Human life is too short for one
person to be able to deal with too many things in turn. A
division of the sciences had to take place, and then still
further specialization within each of them. These are
practical reasons, marginal in a certain sense. The essential
thing is - here again the strictly selective aspectness of our
cognition is heard from - that in order to successfully
acquire knowledge of something we must simultaneously resign
from the cognition of an infinite possible number of things.
The expansion of information is based on constantly narrowing
possibilities. Strict asceticism is a necessary condition for
any progress whatsoever. The modern natural science owe all
of their success to the fact that - in sharpening their method
- they abandoned the majority of questions posed by medieval
metaphysics; they limited themselves to the investigation of
the mathematical structure of reality. Mathematics turned out
to be the language by which one can impart experience.
Mathematicized empiricism became precisely that aspect beyond
which the empirical sciences could not go under the threat of
losing their identity.

The stratification of the planes of religious and
scientific cognition is hence not a tactical manoeuvre, but
necessary as resulting from the nature of things. The loss of
identity carries the threat of schizophrenia, except that in a
certain sense it is the reverse of what occurs in mental
illnesses: the stratification of planes is a sign of
normality, whereas efforts at their unification - a symptom of
a split in the methodological personality. A mixing of aspects
leads to distortions, all the worse for not being subject to
treatment by any medicine.

If my metaphysical digression is correct, a certain
stratification of cognitive planes will last as long as our
mind remains immersed in the one-dimensional stream of time.

5. Towards a Synthesis.

But does this stratification of planes always have to
be as drastic as at present? Can two planes remain separate
and still approach each other? Perhaps they can approach each

other asymptotically so as to completely merge at the boundaries (in the temporal plus infinity)?

Already today one can see signs of a certain rapprochement. I detect it in the following phenomena among others:

1) The unusual fruitfulness of the so-called frontier problems arising at the meeting point of various scientific disciplines. Often cited as an example here is cybernetics, which was born from an exchange of thoughts and common discussions among mathematicians, physicists, physiologists, philosophers, and jurists. In the very names: astrophysics, physical chemistry, biochemistry, biophysics one can see the interdisciplinary origin of these sciences. The general theory of systems – a promising field of investigation – is an attempt at a systematic search for common denominators of even very far-removed fields and their combination into a coherent "supersystem". In the general theory of systems some thinkers see either the inspiration for, or the realization of, the philosophy of the future.

Many more similar examples and tendencies in modern scientific circles could be cited.

2) The rapid development of so-called meta-sciences, or various kinds of sciences of scinces: from more ore less successful attempts to systematize the collection of practical directions concerning the organization of scientific work, the psychology and sociology of science, various kinds of theories of scientific cognition, all the way up to very abstract, purely formal works aiming at the reconstruction of the logical structure of some scientific theory in a certain moment of its development (synchronic models) or also in the evolution of a given theory in time (diachronic models).

3) A certain group of meta-sciences – or, perhaps more precisely, some of their branches – dealing with the discovery and analysis of the assumptions (primarily tacit) on which the individual sciences are based. Sciences of this kind (or also sets of problems of this kind) can be called "sub-sciences". So, for example, among the tacit assumptions of the modern empirical sciences are mentioned: the possibility of describing nature through mathematical functions (the mathematicalness of nature); a certain "uniformity" of nature which is more or less the same as was earlier expressed in the saying: "natura non facit saltus" (nature does not make leaps) and what can be expressed more modernly by stating that nature is described (in good approximation) by mathematical functions simple enough for man to be able to understand it; etc. Since these problems are very specialized, we only mention them and

refer those interested to the professional literature. Of sole importance for us is the assertion that one can speak of a certain kind of synthesis of the sciences "from below" (or perhaps a trend towards such synthesis), manifesting itself in the discovery and methodological reconstruction of assumptions common to scientific theories often very far distant from each other.

4) The development of science is governed by – as we have seen several times in the previous chapters – a certain inner logic. Modern philosophy of science tries to uncover and understand this logic. Science – understood either as a system or as an institutional creation – is distingished by relative autonomy and a certain capacity for self-organization. Today one can observe a growth in the complexity of the structure of science, on the one hand, and a growth of its integration on the other. The growth of specialization is accompanied by a growth in feed-backs between ostensibly separate fields. The network of feed-backs branching out ever further, more and more complicates the structure of science, but at the same time it more and more closely unites it. A superficial paradox: unity is achieved through differentiation.

All of the above-described unifying mechanisms operate within the structure of the empirical sciences. Will they someday extend to the humanities? Will they extend beyond the plane of the sciences and also include the plane of philosophy and the plane of theology? Undoubtedly trends towards merger create a favorable climate for great syntheses. But do such syntheses – true syntheses and not only syntheses that spring from the poetic spirit – have real chances? If the considerations of the previous paragraph are correct, then aspectness is a necessary and unavoidable feature of human cognition; it is a consequence of the fact that if we cognize anything at all, we cognize it in time.

Perhaps symbiosis is a temporary synthesis; a synthesis along the way.

6. Synthesis.

The stratification of cognition appears to be a necessary feature of cognition itself. But it is man who cognizes. And in him all of these layers should arrange themselves harmoniously. In the opposite case, man's personality is threatened. The stratification of the personality signifies advanced deviation from psychic norm. However, the matter here does not merely concern psychology.

It also concerns honesty, above all towards oneself. Contradictory beliefs can be maintained - assuming psychic normality - only at the cost of sacrificing the most elementary ethical principles.

Here sythesis is indispensable. All of the cognitive planes should make up the personality of a maturely thinking individual. After all, it is the same man who cognizes the world, discovers the laws of nature, constructs the edifice of science, and it is the same man who in answer to the summons directed to himself says "I believe". A clash occurs between this summons and the store of knowledge acquired by man. The cognized, classified, investigated, predicted contends with the Unknowable. Cognitive planes criss-cross. The mind enters the area of tensions and potential conflicts. These are not solely conflicts of a purely cognitive nature, questions to which the curiosity of the world enjoins us to seek answers. These are questions on which the existence of man depends, existential problems in the deepest sense of this world. And precisely for that reason the synthesis of planes should take place on the "hyper-plane" of the existential concerns of man.

It should be always in the process of becoming and not be made, for this synthesis - in our present situation, the situation of beings immersed in the stream of time - is never something finished. It is a process, a movement towards ...

From this movement the present notes were born.

Recapitulation

Pilate touched the root of the problem. But the question "what is truth?" can have many shades of meaning: from the destructive note of scepticism (is truth at all possible?) all the way to rhetorical self-confidence (what is truth? why this, of course!). Both the philosophy of science as well as some theological trends are closer to the sceptical tone of Pilate himself.

However, neither in the philosophy of science can the concept of truth be replaced by verifiability nor in the field of faith can truthfulness of what is believed in be replaced by committal of the effects of faith.

Religious belief must be rational. One can make a blind committal, without giving any reasons at all, only to rationality.

The rationality of beliefs is connected with their truthfulness. The impartation of what we recognize as truth is the essential function of language, but truth itself cannot be reduced to grammatical rules. At a certain moment one must break through the enchanted circle of syntax and somehow come to reality.

But religious beliefs are not only the result of cold calculation, and in this respect they differ essentially from scientific convictions. Scientific information is located "outside" the scientist; it can be easily isolated from his personal problems. Religious belief absorbs, enfolds the believer; it is his existential concern. And this is precisely what committal is. But rational reasons should precede committal. In order to be worthy of man, committal must be rational.

One of the important features of rationality is the striving for synthesis. Meanwhile, the stratification of levels of cognition (cognition through science, cognition through faith, and others) is an accomplished fact. The observance of competencies and remaining within one's own territory is a condition of symbiosis. Today one can state without hesitation that open faith and honest science can live in symbiosis. This is a great step forward in comparison with the previous period of mutual aversion and notorious misunderstandings.

The possibility of a symbiosis of science and faith is not only the result of the accelerated process of the maturation of theology, its ever greater openness to the changes caused by the development of science. It is also a contribution of science itself. The science of today, giving rise to the feeling of mystery and the feeling of participation in it, as it were, opens our mentality to a reality which surpasses us, but of which we are a part. These are oftentimes almost religious feelings or, in any case, paving the way for religious feelings.

In science itself the longing for synthesis always lay dormant. Today the signs of this longing are stronger than ever before. One can detect them (a) in the extraordinary fruitfulness of problems arising at the meeting point of various sciences (so-called frontier problems), (b) in the rapid development of meta-sciences and (c) "sub-sciences" or sciences dealing with the discovery and analysis of assumptions on which these sciences are based, (d) in the growth of integration of the broadly conceived system of science. Will these unifying mechanisms, operating within the structure of the empirical sciences, also extend to the humanities? Will they someday include philosophy and theology?

Without doubt all of these trends create a favorable climate for great synthesis. But there is no way back: a future synthesis, if it ever takes place, cannot return to the mixing of planes and the renewed confusion of cognitive strata. Similarly, the synthesis presently taking place in the psyche of the believing scientist (or more generally - in the psyche of every believer who is familiar with the modern sciences) cannot occur at the cost of mixing separate levels.

All of this indicates that selectivity (aspectness) is an unavoidable feature of human cognition.

It may be that as long as our mind is immersed in the one-dimensional stream of time the only synthesis possible for us is a continually improving, but still only, symbiosis.

A symbiosis which is a synthesis along the way.

Sixteen:

Faith and Existence

This book has no ending. It cannnot have. To be sure, this last chapter is evidence of having completed a certain stage of thinking, but only a certain stage. Reflections will continue to live on and mature for as long as rational reflection on the content of life is possible.

I look back and run through the previous chapters in my mind. And the questions arises: why all of this? Perhaps this is just a normal reaction; an impulse of dejection after the stress connected with a long period of intense work, when one can suddenly see its end clearly. But perhaps the meaning of this doubt goes deeper, perhaps it is an echo of the statement once made by my interlocutor after a long discussion on the subject of the relation of science to faith: "If the possibility of faith has to be justified by such complicated constructions, then would it not be simpler to merely take up science?" I do not know if my interlocutor was completely serious in making this statement.

For at bottom everyone subcutanously knows that Faith is necessary for life.

The elements of faith cannot be removed either from human culture or from the life of a single individual. Besides, from the moment when man began to walk on two legs these two spheres - the sphere of culture and the sphere of the inner life of the individual - are an organic whole.

Faith in reason lies at the basis of nearly every intended human activity, and especially at the foundations of his scientific activity. Faith in the absoluteness of logic is the "leading idea" of all science, but faith in reason is indispensible for logic not to sink to the level of schematic conventional rules of thinking. Let us repeat the thought expressed in one of the previous chapters: one can only become committed to reason without giving prior reasons.

The postulate of basing one's convictions exclusively on science - aside from the fact that it is hazy and can take on many expressions - is not a judgement of science, but faith directed, in its consequences, against faith in reason.

We believe in reason because it is a value. Faith in reason is only a specific case of faith in values. If we believe in anything at all, we believe because it represents a value for us.

Human language is such that it very often gives various names to the same thing. Another name for faith in reason and faith in value is faith in meaning. Meaning is a condition of reason. Value is a condition of meaning.

The faith of which we speak is a priori to any organized rational thinking, though sometimes very advanced rational thought is required in order to detect the existence of this faith. Just as existence is a priori to thinking ("I exist, therefore I think"), though thinking can be proof of existence ("I think, therefore I am"). This is more than an analogy. Faith is very close to existence. At least in the sense that without faith rational existence is impossible.

However, it sometimes happens that faith changes into experience. Experience in which not the sensory nerve endings react but experience in which one touches not with the hand but with the depth of existence. An encounter in love. Illumination in which one can become lost as in the night. "Thou" ceases to be a word, it takes on meaning. Understanding without explanation. Touching the Absolute.

One can be a non-believer, but if one is at least something of a man, then one experiences such faith, and sometimes such experience. Perhaps such faith and such experience are already religious faith in embryo, but it is certain that religious faith grows out of such faith and such experience.

The one who has never had experience of man cannot have experience of God.

Religious faith is natural extension of human faith and human experience. A logic which would only be a product of grey cells and would die along with them would be an illusion

174

rather than logic. Value which did not transcend a conventional agreement, a conditioned reflex or the workings of the endocrine glands, would be completely valueless. The meaning of everything identically ending with non-existence would not differ meaningfully from senselessness. Love would remain, perhaps, the only human value in the irrational and senseless world. If a mechanism for extending the species, which even so is fated to die out, could be called a value at all.

Religious faith gives a new dimension to man and the world. It is the dimension of Meaning and Value. Without Meaning there are no grounds, and that is why this dimension is a reason in and of itself.

"If the possibility of faith has to be justified by such complicated constructions, then would it not be simpler to merely take up science?"

The point is that the possibility of faith does not have to be justified by any constructions. The possibility of faith is a requirement of existence. And only living in a world of Value and Meaning is truly worth taking up science.

Footnotes

Chapter 1.

(1) K. R. Popper, The Rationality of Scientific Revolutions, Clarendon Press, Oxford 1975, pp. 72 - 101.

(2) The working class as a social group formed in the seventeenth and eighteenth centuries. From the very outset it formed beyond the territory controlled by the Church structures. Hence, strictly speaking, the Church never lost the working class. Not until the nineteenth century and at the beginning of the twentieth century did the Church discover the new continent and take up the task of its Christianization.

(3) Science and Religious Belief - A Selection of Recent Historical Studies, ed. by C. A. Russell, Universuty of London Press - The Open University Press, 1973.

Chapter 2.

(1) See the chapter "Science contemporaine et foi Chretienne - Nouvelle position d'un ancien probleme" in the book by Jean Ladrière, La science, le monde et la foi, Casterman, 1972. Some thoughts presented below are taken from Ladrière.

(2) See A. N. Whitehead, Concept of Nature, Cambridge - At the University Press, 1971, p. 3.

(3) E. Schroedinger, What Is Life? - Mind and Matter, Cambridge - At the University Press, 1969, pp. 127 - 128.

(4) W. Van Orman Quine, From a Logical Point of View, Harvard University Press, Cambridge - Massachusetts, 1964.

Chapter 3.

(1) K. Rahner, Vom Glauben inmitten der Welt, Herder, 1962.
(2) New York 1969.
(3) Op. cit.
(4) According to information theory, the processes leading to the reduction of entropy (and hence to ordering) create information.

Chapter 4.

(1) Science and Religious Belief - A selection of Recent Historical Studies, ed. by C. A. Russell, University of London Press - The Open University Press, 1973.
(2) Moses and Atomism, pp. 5 - 19, in (1).
(3) H. Butterfield, The Origins of Modern Science, London 1949.
(4) Merton Revisited, or Science and Society in the Seventeenth Century, pp. 55 - 73, in (1).
(5) The Christian Doctrine of Creation and the Rise of Modern Natural Science, pp. 294 - 315, in (1).
(6) Descartes excluded teleological causes from the field of scientific investigations simply for the reason that "God's purposes are not to be investigated".
(7) Published by Scottish Academic Press, 1972.
(8) The Grand Design - A New Physics, pp. 102 - 130, in (1).
(9) E. A. Burtt, The Metaphysic of Newton, pp. 131 - 146, in (1).
(10) Newton often called his mechanics "natural philosophy".
(11) Polemic with S. Clarke, First Letter of Leibniz.
(12) The problem of "corrections" is discussed in greater detail by D. Kubrin, Newton and the Cyclical Cosmos: Providence and the Mechanical Philosophy, pp. 147 - 169, in (1). Different interpretation of this problem see M. Heller and A. Staruszkiewicz, A Physicist's View on the Polemics between Leibniz and Clarke, Organon, 11 (1975) 205 - 213.

(13) See D. Cairne, Thomas Chalmer's Astronomical Discourses: A Study in Natural Theology, pp. 195 - 204, in (1).

(14) See J. Dillenberger, The Apologetic Defence of Christianity, pp. 170 - 194, in (1).

Chapter 5.

(1) Penguin Books, 1975 (first edition in 1936). The book contains a modernizing introduction written by the author in 1946.

(2) Other important books by the same author: The Foundations of Empirical Knowledge; Philosophical Essays; The Problem of Knowledge; The Concept of Person; The Origins of Pragmatism; Metaphysics and Common Sense; "Russell and More: The Analytic Heritage; The Central Questions of Philosophy; Probability and Evidence.

(3) H. Reichenbach, The Rise of Scientific Philosophy, University of California Press, 1951, chapter 17.

(4) It is worth noting that A. Zinoviev constructed a logically consistent theory of meaning in which meaningfulness does not coincide with verifiability. For example, the statement "A round rectangle bears the name feldfebel" has meaning; it is "understandable" but is neither true nor false; see A. Zinoviev, Logika nauki (The Logic of Science), Warszawa 1976, p. 89.

Chapter 6.

(1) Polish translation: Polish Scientific Publishers, Warsaw 1972; English edition 1964.

(2) See the monograph: S. W. Hawking, G. F. R. Ellis, The Large scale Structure of Space-Time, Cambridge - At the University Press, 1973.

(3) Ibid. p. 364.

(4) D. Bonhoeffer, Widerstand und Ergebung. Briefe und Aufzeichnungen aus der Haft, Herausgegeben von Eberhard Bethge, 1965.

Chapter 7.

(1) J. Monod, Le hasard et la necessite - Essai sur la philosophie naturelle de la biologique moderne. Édition du

Seuil. First edition in 1970, p. 175. All quotes in this chapter come from this book.

(2) See the remarks on the subject of entropy at the beginning of the third chapter.

(3) If this chapter were written today (May 1986), Monod's remarks would be supplemented with at least some comments concerning newest achievements in the field of thermodynamics of irreversible processes; see, for instance, I. Prigogine, I. Stengers, Order out of Chaos, Bantam Books, 1984.

Chapter 8.

(1) Knowledge and Belief, Oxford University Press, 1973. All quotes in the present chapter are from this book.

Chapter 9.

(1) R. J. Ackermann, Belief and Knowledge, Macmillan, 1973.

(2) See pp. 40 - 50 in Ackermann's book and nearly all of the footnotes to chapter three of this book. Above I have merely given the structure of the lottery paradox. Its paradoxicality is more apparent in juxtaposition with the remaining criteria of rationality of belief accepted by Ackermann.

Chapter 10.

(1) M. Morawski, Wieczory nad Lemanem, Krakow 1902.

(2) Perhaps in the Anglo-Saxon countries the situation is somewhat different. Some theologians of that language region are not unacquainted with the achievements of the philosophy of science and the philosophy of language.

(3) B. J. F. Lonergan, Method in Theology, Longman and Todd, Darton, chapter 4, sec. 7.

(4) Vom Glauben inmitten der Welt, Herder, 1962.

(5) Ibid.

(6) Rahner also is not free from this view.

(7) See W. Ross Ashby, An Introduction to Cybernetics, Chapman and Hall, 1958.

(8) K. Rahner, op. cit.

(9) Ibid.

Chapter 11.

(1) A. Einstein, L. Infeld, The Evolution of Physics, Cambridge University Press, 1947.
(2) W. Heisenberg, Physik und Philosophie, S. Hirzel Verlag, Stittgart 1959.
(3) L. Wittgenstein, Philosophische Untersuchungen, Blackwell and Mott, 1958.
(4) Ibid.

Chapter 12.

(1) S. K. Langer, Philosophy in a New Key - A Study in the Symbolism of Reason, Rite, and Art (Polish edition, Warszawa 1976).
(2) The theory of sign in such a context can be constructed in a very precise manner. E.g. A. Zinoviev takes the theory of sign, constructed by himself, as the point of departure for entire logic; see his "The Logic of Science" (Polish edition: Warsaw 1976).
(3) S. K. Langer, op. cit.
(4) See e.g. E. Nagel, The Structure of Science, Harcourt, Brace World, 1961.
(5) S. K. Langer, op. cit.
(6) Ibid.
(7) A. D. Ritchie, The Natural History of Mind (1936), cited by S. K. Langer, op. cit.
(8) Symbole donne a penser, Esprit 8, 1959.
(9) See chapter 1, sec. 2.
(10) See chapter 1, sec. 6.
(11) For more specialized considerations of the symbolic nature of theological language see: J. Ladrière, La discours theologique et le symbole, Revue des Sciences Religieuses 49, 1975; J. Ladrière, Langage theologique et philosophie analitique, Archive di Filosofia, Roma, 1974.

Chapter 13.

(1) F. Chapey, Science et foi - affrontement de deux langages, Éd. du Centurion, 1974. All quotes in the present chapter are from this book.
(2) See chapter 1.

Chapter 14.

(1) Polish translation: Ed. Pax, Warszawa 1977.
(2) In the second part of his philosophical activity
Wittgenstein rather radically changed his views. His initial
views (the so-called First Wittgenstein) are contained in the
"Tractatus Logico-Philosophicus", whereas "Philosophical
Investigations" ("Philosophische Untersuchungen") are
characteristic of the second period (The Second Wittgenstein).
(3) These are students' notes from Wittgenstein's
lectures published in 1938 (ed. C. Barrett, Oxford 1966).
(4) See chapter 11.
(5) Éd. du Cerf, Paris 1974.
(6) This is the famous seventh (last) thesis of the
"Tractatus".
(7) A. Lagache, op. cit, p. 58.
(8) L. Wittgenstein, Carnets 1914 - 1916; French
edition: Ed. Gallimard, 1971.
(9) Mrs. Lagache, I trust, will forgive me for
oversimplyfing - and perhaps distorting - her arguments.
Otherwise, they are very interesting arguments, especially in
those passages which concern the problem of the meaning of the
world and the meaning of life. It would be worth returning to
them at some other time.
(10) K. R. Popper, Objective Knowledge - An
Evolutionary Approach, Clarendon Press, Oxford 1975, p. 44.
(11) Ibid. p. 319.
(12) R. Trigg, op. cit. chapter 4.
(13) For interesting remarks on the subject of the
stipulation for expanding the area of rationality see: J.
Ladrière, Les enjeux de la rationalite, Ed. Aubier-Montaigne,
1977 (especially pp. 193 - 196). The author stipulates the
extension of rationality from science to the fields of ethics
and art.

Chapter 15.

(1) The above is true as far as the so-called
"classical singularities" are concerned. It is not known at
present whether the more realistic theory of quantum gravity
will remove singularities, or not.
(2) The basic work on the subject of singularities is
the monograph: S. W. Hawking, G. F. R. Ellis, The Large Scale
Structure of Space-Time, Cambridge, At the University Press,
1973.

Name Index

183

Philosophy in Science

ISSN 0277-2434

Editors: M. Heller, W. R. Stoeger, S.J., J. M. Zycinski

Center for Interdisciplinary Studies of the Vatican Observatory, Castel Gandolfo, of the Pontifical Academy of Theology, Cracow, and of the Pachart Foundation, Tucson.

One of the most dangerous movements of traditional philosophy has been its attempt to develop philosophical analyses independently of scientific results. And one of the most hopeless illusions of nineteenth century science was its desire to replace philosophy by science and to give physical answers to questions posed in classical philosophy. Nowadays, being more conscious of methodological restrictions, we have a chance to avoid both false alternatives and to develop philosophical thinking in the context of scientific achievements. **Philosopy in Science** aims to foster the development and understanding of philosophical questions as they are encountered within the sciences and seeks to promote mutually enriching dialog at the professional level among scientists, philosophers and philosophers of science.

Volume 1. Stoeger: The evolving interaction between philosophy and the sciences: towards a self-critical philosophy. Kisiel: Techne, logos, gnosis. Von Weizsaecker: Greek philosophy and modern physics. Barbour: Philosophical principles and the problem of motion. Heller: A comment on Lorentz invariance. Park: A model of irreversible behavior. Rayski: A philosophy of quantum mechanics. Chylinski: Operationalism and fundamental models of physics. Zycinski: The relationship between science and philosophy in dialectical materialism. $ 28.00

Volume 2. Heller: The meaning of meaning. Del Re: Aquinas vs. epistemological criticism: a case for philosophy in science. Piro: Processes, substances, and Leibniz's epistemology: a case for essentialism in contemporary physics. Janik: An attempt at interpretation of the Thomistic hylomorphic theory in view of contemporary physics. Zycinski: Falsification and discomfirmation in cosmology. Stoeger and Heller: A causal interaction constraint on the initial singularity? Haman: On the objectivity of the laws of physics. Pienkowski: Probability and epistemology. Voise: The drama of Galileo, the past and the present. $ 28.00

Pachart Publishing House
(Pachart Foundation, A Nonprofit Association)
1130 San Lucas Circle
Tucson, Arizona 85704

The Astronomy Quarterly

ISSN 0364-9229

Editor: Peter D. Usher
Associate Editors: R. D. Chapman, M. Heller
Editorial Board: A. H. Delsemme, D. H. DeVorkin, J. E. Felten, G. Gale,
M. S. Giampapa, E. R. Harrison, A. A. Hoag, W. M. Liller,
D. E. Osterbrock, L. G. Taff, G. A. Wegner, M. Zeilik II.

The Astronomy Quarterly examines the role of astronomy, especially cosmology, in natural philosc and in culture in general, as well as astronomy's influence upon the intellectual atmosphere of the epoch. The Astronomy Quarterly features in-depth, non-technical articles written by professional scientists, philosophers and historians of science for the educated layman and student.

Issue 1. Serkowski: Should we search for planets around stars? Day: Interstellar silicates. Collins: Some reflections on the sources of energy in extragalactic objects. Whitaker: De facie in orbe Lunae. Craine: Visiting American astronomical facilities, I. Southern Arizona.

Issue 2. Culver and Ianna: Astrology and the scientific method. I. The nature of astrological planetary influences. Boeshaar: Chemical evolution in galaxies. Norton: An early Gregorian telescope. News Notes.

Issue 3. Culver and Ianna: Astrology and the scientific method - II. Astrological experimentation and prediction. Whitaker: De facie in orbe Lunae. Taff: Stellar systems and gravity - what do we know? Reflections/Refractions.

Issue 4. Imhoff: In search of the T Tauri stars - an historical perspective. Craine: The scale of the universe - Ota-heite 1769. Miller: Optical variability of extragalactic radio sources. Osterbrock: Su-shu Huang. Reflections/Refractions.

Issue 5. Kahn, Pompea, and Culver: Paleoastronomy. Protheroe: Introductory college astronomy - an audio-visual approach. Swihart: The elementary astronomy course at state colleges. White: The relative merits of a sample of recent introductory astronomy textbooks. Reflections/Refractions.

Issue 6. Rudnicki: Are clusters of galaxies individuals? Whitaker: De facie in orbe Lunae. Reed: Is the Stonehenge heel stone a sun god? Pacholczyk: Ten years of studies of 'related objects'. Reflections/Refractions.

Subscription rates (US$ per four issues): $ 22.00 domestic, $ 27.00 foreigh. Back issues: $ 25.00 each for issues 1 through 8, if available, $ 5.00 each for issues beginning with issue 9.

Pachart Publishing House
(Pachart Foundation, A Nonprofit Association)
1130 San Lucas Circle
Tucson, Arizona 85704

The Astronomy Quarterly Library

General Editor: R. B. Culver

ENCOUNTERING THE UNIVERSE
Michael Heller. Translated by J. Potocki. Edited by G. W. Collins, II
A collection of essays on cosmology and its philosophical
ramifications. It examines the very old philosophical problem of man's
existence within the Universe in the light of modern cosmology.
(The Astronomy Quarterly Library, Volume 2)
ISBN 0-912918-07-1
$ 9.95

AN AMATEUR RADIO TELESCOPE
George W. Swenson, Jr.
Intended for amateur astronomers, radio "hams", electronic hobbyists
and college students in astronomy, physics and electrical engineering,
this unique book provides the astronomical and electronic background to
enable an intelligent and determined hobbyist to build and operate an
inexpensive radio telescope. The telescope is a phase-switching
interferometer and was built by the author's students. Complete circuit
diagrams and directions are included. Dr. Swenson is Professor of
Astronomy and Electrical Engineering at the University of Illinois,
Urbana-Champaign. "Swenson is thorough; all the information is· there
for the construction of an instrument relying on solid state circuitry"
(D. W. Hughes, in Nature). "His convincing description of practical
problems in construction and operation is clearly based on first-hand
experience and will be most useful to amateurs making a start in
radioastronomy" (J. M. A. Lenihan in Physics Education).
(The Astronomy Quarterly Library, Volume 4)
ISBN 0-912918-06-3
$ 9.95

Pachart Publishing House
(Pachart Foundation, A Nonprofit Association)
1130 San Lucas Circle
Tucson, Arizona 85704

History of Astronomy Series

General Editor: A. G. Pacholczyk

ASTRONOMY BEFORE THE TELESCOPE
Nicholas T. Bobrovnikoff
The work presents a world-wide view of the development of astronomy in various countries with contrasting civilizations (including China and Maya) with emphasis on the interrelationship of its development with other sciences as well as with the political and cultural situations. Volume One: The Earth-Moon System.
(Pachart History of Astronomy Series, Volume 1)
ISBN 0-88126-201-3 $ 38.00

THE EXPANDING UNIVERSE: LEMAÎTRE'S UNKNOWN MANUSCRIPT
M. Heller and O. Godart
A facsimile of an unpublished manuscript intended for the Catholic Encyclopedia of Japan, presents a totality of Lemaître's cosmology as well as his views on the existence of collapsed systems of stars and on the evolution of the Universe.
(Pachart History of Astronomy Series, Volume 2)
ISBN 0-88126-282-X $ 13.00

COSMOLOGY OF LEMAÎTRE
O. Godart and M. Heller
Written by two cosmologists, one of whom was a friend and a close collaborator of Lemaître, the book gives English speaking scientists and historians of science a correct picture of what contemporary science owes to Lemaître.
(Pachart History of Astronomy Series, Volume 3)
ISBN 0-88126-283-8 $ 46.00

Pachart Publishing House
(Pachart Foundation, A Nonprofit Association)
1130 San Lucas Circle
Tucson, Arizona 85704

Astronomy and Astrophysics Series

General Editor: A. G. Pacholczyk

LECTURE NOTES ON INTRODUCTORY THEORETICAL ASTROPHYSICS
R. J. Weymann, T. L. Swihart, R. E. Williams, W. J. Cocke, A. G. Pacholczyk, J. E. Felten, University of Arizona
This volume consists of the expanded lecture notes that have been used by six faculty members of Steward Observatory in a very successful team-teaching course for beginning Astronomy graduate students at the University of Arizona which introduces the students to the important concepts of theoretical astrophysics. It makes an excellent textbook for a survey course in introductory astrophysics at the advanced undergraduate or beginning graduate level. Lecture Notes "...serve to expose students to some of the current concepts in theoretical astrophysics and it retains considerable coherence" (Physics Today).
(Astronomy and Astrophysics Series, Volume 3)
ISBN 0-912918-14-4 $ 15.00

RADIATION TRANSFER AND STELLAR ATMOSPHERES
T. L. Swihart, University of Arizona
Intended to give a good basic understanding of radiation transfer and stellar atmosphere theory to seniors and graduate students, this text has been deliberately kept short, and the attempt was made to keep mathematical accuracy from obscuring physical concepts. This is the third revised and expanded edition of this excellent and widely used text.
(Astronomy and Astrophysics Series, Volume 12)
ISBN 0-912918-18-7 $ 38.00

PLANETARY INTERIORS
V. N. Zharkov, V. P. Trubitsyn, O. Yu. Schmidt Institute of Earth Physics, Moscow. Edited by W. B. Hubbard, University of Arizona
The book presents general conclusions about the structure and composition of the planets of the solar system, based upon discussions of figure and gravitational field, and of the properties and aggregate state of matter in their interiors. "The authors have written a great many papers on high-pressure behavior...and on the theory of figures, and the particular value of this book lies in their bringing together all that and other Russian work and setting it in the context of work done elsewhere" (A. H. Cook in Observatory). "...the book can be profitably used by those who are entering the domain of planetary interiors and who want to avoid the numerous pitfalls well known to

seasoned practitioners of the art. This characteristic gives the book a more permanent value than an up-to-date description of the most recent models could have provided" (R. Smoluchowski, in Astrophysical Letters).
(Astronomy and Astrophysics Series, Volume 6)
ISBN 0-912918-15-2 $ 24.00

THE VIRIAL THEOREM IN STELLAR ASTROPHYSICS
G. W. Collins, II, Ohio State University
This book contains the development and some applications of the virial theorem of classical mechanics. The work is designed to lead the reader from the simplest classical development to the more contemporary applications to collapsed stars and relativistically degenerate configurations. The style is aimed at the graduate student or the professional outside this field.
(Astronomy and Astrophysics Series, Volume 7)
ISBN 0-912918-13-6 $ 19.00

CARBON STARS
Z. K. Alksne and Ya. Ya. Ikaunieks, Radiophysics Observatory of the Latvian Academy of Sciences. Edited by J. H. Baumert, Connecticut College
An extensive summary of information on carbon stars intended for graduate students and researchers on late-type stars. This is an expanded and annotated translation of "Uglerodnye Zvezdy" from Russian. Extensive additions and bibliography bring the material on carbon stars up to date.
(Astronomy and astrophysics Series, Volume 11)
ISBN 0-912918-16-0 $ 24.00

THE SCIENCE OF SPACE-TIME
D. J. Raine, University of Leicester, and M. Heller, Pontifical Academy of Theology, Cracow and Vatican Observatory
An analysis of the development of the space-time structure from Aristotle through Copernicus, Newton, Leibniz and Mach, to the present day relativity and cosmology, looked upon with the eyes of a modern physicist, unveils a remarkable internal logic which almost had to bring Einstein and his General Relativity. The discussion goes beyond the present paradigm of space-time opening broad horizons for physics to come. This interesting and provocative book is unique in its combination of historical background and modern physical approach. It should interest both the historian of science and the relativity theorist, as well as those concerned with the general philosophical structure of modern physical science.
(Astronomy and Astrophysics Series, Volume 9)
ISBN 0-912918-12-8 $ 38.00